SELF-CARE
IS THE NEW
HEALTH-CARE®

Self-Care Is The New Health-Care ®

From Diagnosis to Discovery:
Uncovering the Cause of My Depression Symptoms

Melissa Vance

Published by Garnet Yoga & Wellness © 2016 by Melissa Vance

Self-Care Is The New Health-Care® and Bringing Self-Care To Health-Care® are registered trademarks belonging to Melissa Vance.

The content of this book is for general instruction only. Each person's physical, emotional, and spiritual condition is unique. The instruction in this book is not intended to replace or interrupt the reader's relationship with a physician or other professional. Please consult your doctor for matters pertaining to your specific health and diet.

Printed in the United States of America

ISBN-13: 978-0692691014
ISBN-10: 0692691014

Library of Congress Control Number: 2016906286

Cover design by Rupa Limbu
Cover photo by Lisa Sanders
Back cover photo by Jennifer Bonti
Inside Back Cover Photo by Priscila Camara Photography

Praise

"Melissa Vance, author of *Self-Care Is The New Health-Care* ®, a graduate of the Institute for Integrative Nutrition ® (IIN ®). At IIN ®, she completed a cutting edge curriculum in nutrition and health coaching taught by the world's leading experts in health and wellness. I recommend you read this book and get in touch with Melissa to see how she can help you successfully achieve your goals."

- Joshua Rosenthal, MScED, Founder/Director, Institute for Integrative Nutrition ®

This book is dedicated to the memory of my loving and generous mother,

Shirley Joyce Robison.

Table of Contents

How to Use This Book

This is not an anti-medication book by any means. Prescriptions serve an important purpose, but they are being over-prescribed without looking closer at root causes. It is a HUGE problem that needs to be highlighted and discussed.

This book is a perfect tool for clients who are working with a health coach or other medical professionals. Use it as a guide to lead you toward shifts in your health and overall wellness. This can create powerful changes in mood, weight loss, and vitality. Make notes in this book and/or write in a journal to track your own personal health journey. Make sure to date your answers so you can look back, a few months from now, at all of your incredible progress. You may find over time you have embraced new healthy habits, and you will likely experience a significant transformation toward positive behavior and a more loving view of yourself.

This book is not intended to replace any medical advice. If you have been prescribed any medications, talk with your doctor before stopping or decreasing your dosage.

This book is for anyone wanting more energy, less pain, and a chance for happiness. Those suffering from symptoms of mild depression can use this guide as a stepping stone to happier and healthier living. This book is intended for informational purposes only. It should not be used as a substitute for professional medical advice, diagnosis or treatment. Always consult your professional healthcare provider before beginning or ending any treatment.

Although a long-term cure for depression and anxiety may require counseling, actions such as detoxification, proper nutrition and meditation will help restore the nervous system and neurotransmitters in the brain. These techniques will be discussed in the next few chapters.

For anxiety and stress management, talk to someone. Tell friends, family, and your healthcare providers if you are feeling overwhelmed and let them know how they can help you. If you are considering suicide, please call the 24-hour, toll-free, confidential National Suicide Prevention Lifeline and get help now.

National Suicide Prevention Hotline
1-800-273-TALK (8255)

Experimental Mindset

Try to keep an open mind to each self-care technique as it is presented regardless of your initial reaction to it. An experimental mindset is essential to the process laid out here. If you are not yet ready to drastically change your lifestyle and diet, it's okay! In this case, perhaps you can play around with short-term trials. Find out for yourself what it feels like when you make self-care your first priority. What does it feel like when you eat more vegetables and limit sugar, alcohol, gluten, or dairy products? **Use the Self-Care Check-Ins, placed periodically throughout this book, to evaluate where your focus should be.**

Self-Care Check-In

Use this section to pause and reflect.

Is there someone you would like to dedicate the practice of your self-care to or a goal you wish to achieve with your self-care focus? Describe below:

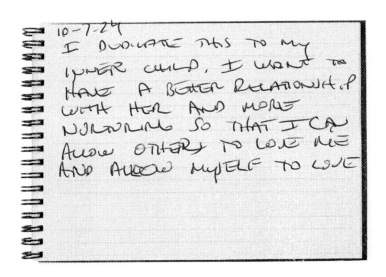

Crowding Out

Since the only things we are adding are self-care techniques, there is no risk of harmful side effects. The good news is that the techniques in this book will not interfere with any of your current medications. Instead, take notice when you are journaling that when you add in healthy routines often there becomes no room for the bad habits.

It's A Marathon, Not A Sprint

Creating powerful shifts in health require a dedicated commitment to actively choose self-care. Let's not forget about the classic lesson of the tortoise and the hare. The turtle won the race with a slow and consistent speed while the rabbit needed a nap before he crossed the finish line. A healthy, happy life is more like an easy-paced marathon, rather than an exhausting, hasty sprint. So start where you are now. Choose realistic, sensible adjustments over what might seem to be instant, shortcut fixes for your health goals.

Choose Self-Care Community

Since we rise by lifting others, a self-care community is a great tool to feel connected and supported during your self-care journey. Use the hashtag **#ChooseSelfcare** to post your inspirational ideas on social media and to connect with others in this self-care journey. If you feel comfortable doing so, you can even share a picture of your Self-Care Check-In journal.

Also, another great way to keep your self-care goals in your mind is to have a #ChooseSelfcare magnet somewhere that you can see periodically throughout the day. You can purchase your magnet from www.ChooseSelfcare.com. I would recommend placing it on your refrigerator or anywhere visible as a gentle reminder to include in your decision-making process.

Introduction

My Mess Is My Message: My Story of Misdiagnosis with Depression

My life was crumbling to pieces, each day, right before my eyes. From the depths of brain fog and fatigue, I struggled daily to find the motivation to just get out of bed. Phone calls from friends went unanswered because I was too tired and felt too lethargic to talk. I just wanted to sleep. I could sleep *all day* and *all night*. The once-fun family activities, like going to the mall or even out to a restaurant, took a terrible toll on me. Next came the phantom pains shooting throughout my body, especially in my hands and legs. I ached all over. Eventually, it was the excessive hair loss, covering my shower floor, which led me to schedule an appointment with my doctor.

It took two weeks to get an appointment with my primary care physician. Then it took a battle through traffic and sitting for 45 minutes past my appointment time in an overcrowded waiting room just to see the nurse about ordering blood work through another facility. FRUSTRATING. After fighting through more traffic to get my blood work completed, I was told it would be ready in another week or so.

When the time came for my follow-up appointment to discuss my blood work findings, I was miserable. The dread and anxiety had built up so much that I was flying off the handle at my loved ones and chewing on the skin around my lips and fingers. I was so close to a mental breakdown that I went to my follow-up appointment convinced that I had some form of cancer or other horrible illness. Whatever diagnosis they delivered, I was determined to accept my fate. I just wanted the comfort of knowing what my condition was called. Sitting for an agonizing 38 minutes in the waiting room, finally I was called in to speak with the doctor.

I held my breath as I sat down. The doctor smiled and said, "Your blood work and vitals look good. You're in great health."

REALLY? I said, "NO, that can't be right. There has got to be something wrong with me. I want my life back."

He asked me a series of routine questions from a form. He never looked me in the eye. They were questions about my sleep patterns, stress levels, and my energy. (He never asked me anything about what I eat, do for exercise, or activities to manage stress). He only spoke to me for about 10 minutes before the word "depression" came out of his mouth. He explained, "You have all of the signs." There it was, depression. Not cancer or one of the other horrible diseases I had imagined. It seemed surreal.

He diagnosed me with depression and gave me a prescription for Lexapro along with several free samples of the drug. He urged me to start taking the drug immediately; "These will get you started," he directed. "It could take up to six weeks before the medication will deliver the full effect, so you should go ahead and begin taking them right now."

Reading the long list of possible side-effects (including anxiety), sent my anxiety through the roof.

Most Common Side Effects of Antidepressants:
- **Nausea**
- **Increased Appetite & Weight Gain**
- **Loss of Sexual Desire & Other Sexual Problems**
- **Fatigue & Drowsiness**
- **Insomnia**
- **Dry Mouth**
- **Blurred Vision**
- **Constipation**
- **Dizziness**
- **Agitation**
- **Irritability**
- **Anxiety**

The doctor finished speaking. I sat there, with a blank stare. I was speechless. I could only nod my head. If you knew me, you'd know—I always have something to say. Not this time. I was in *complete shock*. I dropped the antidepressants into my purse. Stunned, I went home and cried.

I thought hard about it. *This can't be happening to me. There's no way its depression. Maybe I'm a little sad because the exhaustion and constant pain are extremely overwhelming. But it's not like I want to kill myself, or anything so drastic.* My gut instinct told me, *Get another opinion.* I did.

I received a referral from a friend. This time I chose the natural and holistic route. I scheduled an appointment with a nutrition expert, and went through my list of symptoms, *again*.

I mentioned the first doctor's diagnosis and prescription for Lexapro. She looked me in the eyes, with compassion. I felt as if I were being listened to for the first time in ages. What a *relief!* She asked me what foods I ate and how much water I drank daily.

"I don't believe you're depressed," she told me. "But something is causing these symptoms and we need to find the root of the problem, not just cover them up." She explained, "If we just keep medicating symptoms with synthetic pills instead of figuring out what is actually causing the problem, it's like treating a bullet wound with a Band-Aid. The problem will never go away and your symptoms will persist indefinitely."

This made amazing sense to me.

The next question my new holistic practitioner asked me was about antibiotics. This question cracked the mystery wide open. For the past year and a half, I had been prescribed antibiotics for sinus infections almost every six to eight weeks. The result? I had developed a severe candida yeast overgrowth.

This overgrowth was causing the brain fog, pain, hair loss, fatigue, anxiety, and other depression-like symptoms. The processed food I had been eating was also contributing to the candida invasion. The combination made things worse and produced cravings for sugary junk food. This, in turn lead to the development of inflammation inside my body.

Taking an antidepressant, without looking at the contributing factors, would not have helped at all. Instead, it would have further complicated the problem. It turns out, antidepressants are one of the *most* overly prescribed medications in today's society, second only behind antibiotics according to the Mayo Clinic.[1]

The various signs of depression I had been exhibiting were symptoms of something much greater going on. The combination of the candida issue, lack of exercise, and eating highly-processed food, was creating immense turmoil within my gut. The disruption in my gut created a significant decrease in serotonin (the happy hormone).

I spent the next few months detoxing and doing a strict Candida Cleanse diet, which we will discuss later in this book. After I completed the cleanse, I began watching my diet and taking a combination of different supplements to get my immune system back on track. After a few months, my family witnessed a metamorphosis. Along with my smile, my energy returned. Instead of needing to lay in bed all day, I went to the gym. I not only had my health back, but I gained a new purpose.

A paradigm shift had happened for me. By going through such a personal health crisis, I became a seeker of knowledge. I was *hungry* for nutrition information and an increased understanding of root causes for many common health concerns. Sharing my story with others made me realize how many people out there were suffering. It became clear to me why I had experienced such an ordeal. I was supposed to be a voice for those who could not speak up.

The next few steps of my journey lead me to completing the program at the Institute for Integrative Nutrition®, becoming a Drugless Practitioner and furthering my certifications in yoga training through Asheville Yoga Center. This is how I turned my mess into my message. I wanted to share my story and help educate others on the importance of self-care.

Once I saw behind the curtain of our healthcare system, I witnessed how truly broken it is. I now realize the tendency toward medicating without seeking root causes is out of control. It is leading us into a downward spiral of decreasing health. Over time, our society tends to accept this as a normal part of aging. Accepting this line of thought teaches our children to become dependent on pharmaceuticals, and thus begins the vicious cycle of adverse reactions and more prescriptions.

In the United States alone, $8,000 per person is spent annually on healthcare.[2] Self-care provides an alternative, low-cost solution to a high-cost problem.

I must reiterate here, I am not against medication. Prescriptions serve an important purpose, but they are being over-prescribed without looking closer at root causes or at the reactions they create in the body.

Many people who are prescribed antidepressants (and many other medications) are not responding to these drugs. Antidepressants have been known to over-promise and under-deliver. They are then given more prescriptions, on top of what they are currently taking.
This can cause them to experience other health concerns, besides continuing to suffer from mild depression. Meanwhile, the depression itself is a symptom of an underlying, undiagnosed condition. At this point, not only do they still have their original problem, but now they have additional health issues, which further complicates the discovery and treatment of the root cause.

It is time we stepped off the hamster wheel to nowhere. We must address the culprits which bring about the various depression symptoms, like those from which I suffered.

In addition to, and often in lieu of, offering prescriptions to their patients, our healthcare professionals need to be able to offer nutritional counseling. The reality is, many health problems can be addressed or completely reversed by better nutritional habits and self-care choices.

There needs to be a new health-care standard. The best way to heal the mind is to heal the body as a whole. Since prescribing vegetables and natural solutions will never be more profitable than prescribing synthetic drugs, we simply have to take responsibility for invoking the smarter concept of self-care is the new health-care®.

Self-Care Check-In

Now it is time for our first Self-Care Check-In. In the following journal, share your own story of your struggles and successes thus far. Or if you do not know where to start, write down a few thoughts or feelings that come to mind after you read about my journey. These thoughts will provide interesting context as we delve deeper.

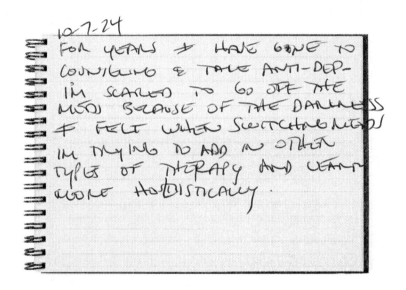

10-7-24

FOR YEARS I HAVE GONE TO COUNSELING & TAKE ANTI-DEP- IM SCARED TO GO OFF THE MEDS BECAUSE OF THE DARKNESS I FELT WHEN SWITCHING MEDS IM TRYING TO ADD IN OTHER TYPES OF THERAPY AND LEARN MORE HOLISTICALLY.

Step 1:

Self-Reflection

Chapter 1:
The Importance of Self-Care

Many of us tend to provide for our families to the detriment of our own health and self-care. This seems to be the new normal. We engage in long hours at work, always rushing from place to place. There never seems to be enough time to relax. Eventually, extended neglect for our wellbeing leads to major health problems and unhappiness. What did all of this suffering bring us? Was the bigger house or expensive car worth it? Is chronic sickness and unhappiness a necessary consequence of "keeping up with the Joneses?"

Your health is your most valuable asset, not your stocks, bonds, house, or 401k. What are you doing to invest in your health for the future?

The answer is No. Our children watch us as we give of ourselves until we become depleted and sick. That is how the cycle repeats itself when they become parents. It is how they have been trained. They recreate our behaviors by watching our actions and decisions. This is called the vicious cycle of self-ruin, and it repeats every generation. However, there is a solution we can use to bring this cycle to an end. It is called self-care.

When we board an airplane flight, the flight attendants always give a demonstration on how to use the oxygen masks, in case the plane loses cabin pressure. They *always* stress the importance of securing your own personal mask before assisting those with whom you are traveling.

When faced with a dangerous situation, what do you think most parents do instinctively? You guessed it. They rush to put the mask on their children before securing their own mask. The reason flight attendants instruct us in this way is if the oxygen quickly rushes out of the cabin before you have your mask secured, you could pass out. Children and the elderly will either not be capable of helping you or not know how. If the same scenario happened and you already had your oxygen mask in place, you could then successfully assist your family, and others in need. The same mindset applies to self-care. We must take care of ourselves first, in order to best take care of those we love.

Self-care is an action (extreme or subtle) that we can engage in, on a regular basis, to reduce stress and maintain our health and wellbeing. Self-care can mean many different things to different people. One of the main reasons self-care is not taken as seriously as it should be is the perception that self-care is extravagant or selfish. Massages, nail appointments, health retreats, and other "pampering," are all forms of self-care. These are fine, if your budget allows, but they are not the foundational types of self-care we are spotlighting here.

Getting a nice pampering massage every day would be great. But if we are drinking soda all day and mentally attacking ourselves with negative self-talk, then we are counteracting any positive steps we started, getting nowhere fast. The type of self-care we need to focus on is the type that holds us accountable for our current mental, physical, and emotional states.

"you can not pour from an empty cup"

An excellent definition of self-care is the actions that people take on their own to focus on and maintain their health on a day-to-day basis as well as to avoid illness. These actions can refer to anything from hygiene, nutrition, physical activity, thought processes, or even one's surroundings. It can be thought of as taking responsibility for one's own self. Daily self-care choices are critical for the difference between a good or bad day. It can also be a difference between vibrant, healthy living and chronic disease. For most of us, self-care is an afterthought, at best, or worse, something we completely neglect.

It is time to make self-care a priority! Self-care is about paying attention to our physical, mental, and emotional needs. The ailments we experience are our body's way of sending us messages, asking that we take better care of ourselves.

If we ignore these messages and continue the abusive, thoughtless behavior, it will eventually lead to burn-out and possibly allow illness and disease to take hold.

Good self-care routines are aligned with preventative medicine and could reverse some health issues. It is not selfish to refill your own "cup" so you can pour into others'. It is not just a luxury; rather, it is essential to our wellbeing and to the prosperity of the people we love.

By making our own self-care a priority, we are decreasing our risk for depression and disease. To experience positive results, a person does not have to go to extremes, overturning every aspect of his or her life. Subtle shifts toward self-care habits can cause a ripple effect in all facets of one's life: at work, at home with the family, and even with one's mind and emotions.

Make self-care a priority in your life by creating your own system. Use the "S.Y.S.T.E.M." acronym: **S**aves **Y**ou **S**tress **T**ime **E**nergy **M**oney. This sums it up quite nicely. The chances for success are better when there is a plan and routine in place. In order to establish a system, we must become realistic with goals and learn to recognize our own strengths and weaknesses. Let's get started.

Self-Care Check-In

Write down a few of your current strengths and weaknesses pertaining to your wellbeing.

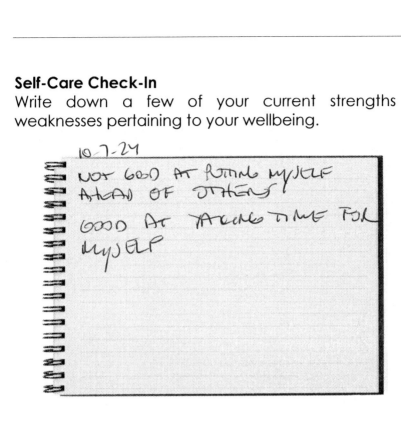

10-7-24

NOT GOOD AT PUTTING MYSELF
AHEAD OF OTHERS

GOOD AT TAKING TIME FOR
MYSELF

Chapter 2: Get Honest

The starting point for designing your own perfect self-care system is awareness. You must be honest with yourself about what works for you and what does not. Then be detailed about experiencing the small changes you make, with awareness in the moment. The goal is to explore your limits, in order to find a more sustainable, middle ground going forward.

The wise philosopher, Socrates, knew how important knowing one's self was in achieving wisdom. It is a great starting point for any goal or transformational process. Understanding your strengths and weaknesses will allow you to navigate around obstacles, so you can achieve whatever goals you set for yourself. In fact, this assessment of the self is essential in creating goals which are achievable and realistic. These will be goals that you will be able to stick with when you come across inevitable challenges.

To know thyself is the beginning of wisdom.
-Socrates

The Institute for Integrative Nutrition®, IIN®, teaches a key concept called Bio-Individuality™, which means that each person has their own unique, highly individualized, nutritional requirements. A Paleo diet might work for your friend, but your own body might require a vegetarian lifestyle to thrive. Some people can feel amazing as they follow a vegan diet, while the same diet causes terrible fatigue and immune dysfunction for others.

This is where self-care is the key to success by listening to the clues our body provides. There is also more to nutrition than just food. What feeds us mentally and spiritually can have as great an impact on our health as the food we choose to eat.

Let's get *honest*. The next few questions will allow you to better understand where your strengths and weaknesses are, so please answer them as honestly as you can. No one will see your answers, unless you choose to share them.

How Balanced is Your Life?

Look at the Circle of Life Exercise on the next page. The circle contains twelve categories which represent important aspects of our lives. This exercise helps us see where we may be off-balance. For example, we may eat a perfectly clean diet, but still feel empty and depressed. Or perhaps the score on the career category is very low, emphasizing what may be triggering our anxiety—signaling an area for us to consider changing for tangible life improvements.

In the first example, we see a person indicating she is extremely pleased with her education. She gave it a rating of ten by placing the dot on the furthest point out on the line. However, look at the next section, career. She does not enjoy her current career and feels stuck in a dead-end job. She therefore gave it a low score by putting the dot closer to the center of the circle.

The experience with her career also reverberates into her financial situation. Her job provides a reasonable salary, but it is not fulfilling. Accordingly, her rating for the financial category falls approximately half-way up the spoke of the wheel.

Scale: 1-3 Suffering/ 4-6 Surviving /7-10 Thriving

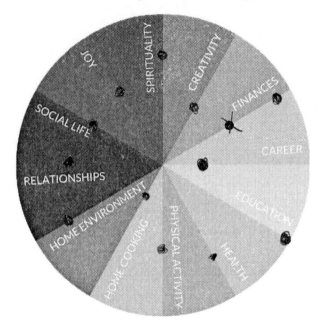

Circle of Life © 2005 Integrative Nutrition Inc. (used with permission)

Your First Circle of Life© Exercise
Completion Date ___10-7-24___

Here is your opportunity to interact, and perhaps learn something new about yourself. We use a zero – ten rating system, with zero being very unsatisfied and ten being completely satisfied. Using the example as your guide, place your rating dot along the spokes of the wheel, from the center of the circle (zero) to the outside of the circle (ten). Rate how gratified you feel now within each category. Make sure you rate all of them, and note the completion date on this exercise for future review.

Scale: 1-3 Suffering/ 4-6 Surviving / 7-10 Thriving

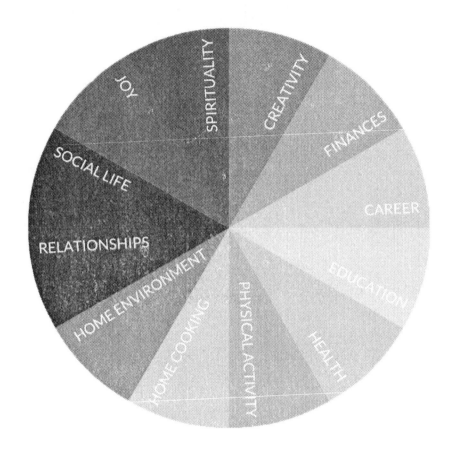

Circle of Life © 2005 Integrative Nutrition Inc. (used with permission)

Now let's analyze your results, and see if we can determine a baseline, from which you can build your own self-care system. It is essential for you to be completely honest with yourself during this exercise. Self-knowledge isn't always happy and perfect. The first step in addressing your life problems, is becoming aware of root causes and the resulting symptoms that bubble up to the surface.

In which three categories did you score the lowest? Remember the Self-Care S.Y.S.T.E.M. as you review your answers. In looking at each of your wheel categories, especially those with the lower scores, what are a few action items that come to mind, which might help you improve your scores?

When choosing self-care action items, choose those that—**S**ave **Y**ou **S**tress, **T**ime, **E**nergy, and **M**oney—**S.Y.S.T.E.M.**

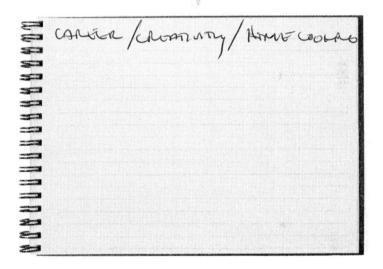

CAREER / CREATIVITY / HOME COOKING

What Pulls You?

Take a moment to think about the last time you chose a healthy self-care option, in relation to some aspect of the Circle of Life. Write about the experience on the next page. What were the different options you could choose? What made you select the healthy one over the others? How did you feel about your choice in that moment, as well as later on in the day?

The Burning Bowl Method

In order to "know thyself" even further, we need to determine what habits, actions, and choices no longer serve our best interests. To begin, get comfortable sitting with your back as straight as possible, in easy pose (cross-legged on the floor or on a meditation bench). If you prefer, you can sit with your legs straight out in front of you. The key is to be comfortable and pain-free, while still holding your spine as tall as possible. This moment presents the perfect opportunity to diffuse an essential oil like lavender, for its calming properties.

Items you need:

- Fireplace, candle, or outside fire pit (any place to SAFELY burn paper)
- Two to seven sheets of paper
- Writing journal
- Box of tissues

Extra items can include:
- Vision board supplies
- Essential Oils

Just Breathe

It is now time for a few cleansing breaths. Inhale through your nose and exhale forcefully, out through your mouth. Force your tongue outward, into what yoga calls "Lion's Breath." Do this a few times, and don't worry if it feels a bit silly. Just let the air in and out. Think about cleansing yourself of negative thoughts and energy as you exhale.

In the Now

Think about what you would like to change in your life, right *now*. Be *very* specific. In your journal, create a list of four particular things you want to focus on transforming. These can be related to the "Circle of Life" quiz from earlier. Describe, in full detail, what you do not like about those things, and how they are negatively affecting your life. Use as many pieces of paper as you need. Really get it all out. Try a stream-of-consciousness style, if this allows the writing to flow more easily. Think about why you want to change these four things.

Offer it to the Fire

Hold the piece(s) of paper in your hand, as you contemplate what you wrote, and why you wrote it. Really take it all in. Grab the tissues, as this can be emotionally raw for some people. How did the items come into your current life? Were they by your choice, or someone else's? Did your goals shift in another direction, after you brought those things in? Are your listed items things you thought you wanted? Did they later not work out the way you had intended?

On your next deep inhalation, tear out and crumple the paper. Hold your breath for a few seconds. On your next exhalation, offer these notes to the fire, and watch them burn. Do you feel a release? Imagine the listed items are burning, and the smoke is carrying them far away, forever. Watch those items disappear as the paper turns to ashes, and they fall away.

Discovering Your Highest Good

Return to the easy-pose posture, and sit quietly. Simply listen to, and feel, your breathing. Inhale slowly and deeply through the nose, and exhale slowly, out the nose. Complete four rounds of this focused breathing to calm and center your mind.

For the next steps, you can choose writing in your journal, or use additional sheets of paper. Now consider four preferable things to replace the items you burned and released. Again, be as specific as you can. Greater detail makes it easier to visualize and bring them to you. Here are a few ideas to spur your thought process:

- **What experiences would help you live your life in alignment with your highest good?**
- **When you think of your highest good, what does it look like?**
- **What do you actually want to experience? Include a description of what that might look or feel like to**

you.

- **Envisioning life improvements you'd like to make, write about the ways others might benefit when you manifest those changes.**
- **Imagine how living with these better situations would look and feel.**

Take all the time you need to write a detailed description of your ideas. As you put voice to them, these thoughts are becoming your intentions and goals. Creating a vision board, with images and symbols of your new intentions, will help keep your goals focused in your awareness for daily action. Once you have finished listing your four new intentions, set them aside for a moment.

Four Steps to a Self-Care System

With a clean sheet of paper, or new page in your journal, write the words, "Four Steps to Accomplishing My Goals."

In this last stage, you'll record four action items which align with the four goals, you set earlier. This breaks up your goals into manageable steps. It's important to keep your action items realistic. They can be subtle changes, or bigger leaps, toward your new goals. If it's more comfortable, you can start small and go slow. As you make progress on your action items, your feelings of accomplishment can fuel further steps forward. Remember, your goals and the related action steps should **S**ave **Y**ou **S**tress, **T**ime, **E**nergy, and **M**oney **(S.Y.S.T.E.M.)**.

As you complete each action step, check it off. Enjoy the victory. No step is too small to celebrate, and the sensation of success is infectious. You will be continually adding more actions to this list.

Once you have achieved one of your steps, and mark it off the list, add the next step. Each one gets you closer to your goals and intentions. You will always have four action items (one for each goal) on your list.

Here is an example to get you started. If my new intention was to quit smoking, my list of "Four Steps" might look like this:

#1 Drink more water
#2 ~~Get nicotine patch~~
#3 Practice yoga daily
#4 Learn meditation
#5 Start savings account with money saved by not purchasing cigarettes

Once I accomplished task #2, I crossed it off and added a #5 to the list. The point here is to focus on only four small steps at a time. This will help to keep our focus on what is important, and allow us to see the consistent progression toward our goals. Each accomplishment is a new opportunity to celebrate victory, regardless of how large or small. Celebrate and bring joy into the process. You are moving ever closer toward a happier and more connected life!

What's Important Now = WIN

I had a high school teacher, who presented the acronym "WIN" to our class. It helped us focus our activity in the classroom. WIN stands for "**W**hat's **I**mportant **N**ow." That little acronym still pops into my mind, whenever I need to assess a challenging situation and keep myself from becoming overwhelmed.

You were likely drawn to this book because you are struggling with difficulties in your health. Perhaps it is something not easily solved. Given the multitude of choices in many situations, learning to prioritize becomes imperative. Frequently, you need only to focus on what's most important in this instant.

If you have tasks or projects piling up, and you are feeling overwhelmed, step back and take a deep breath. Then ask yourself, "What's Important Now?" That's how you WIN. Do this now, and write in your journal, what comes to you.

Which of your concerns can wait until you are more rested, feeling energetic, and in less pain? Write them, along with today's date.

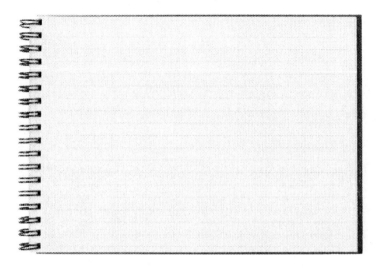

Self-Care S.Y.S.T.E.M.

- Begin where you are, not where you think you should be.
- Start slow, as small changes, over time, lead to big results.
- Celebrate your wins. No victory is too small to rejoice.
- Become a priority in your life.
- Track your progress with a journal
- Revisit the *Circle of Life*© quiz as often as needed to evaluate goals

Now that you have laid a solid foundation for understanding your self-care needs, continue building upon it as you read through the remaining chapters. As you grow and change, so will your self-care maintenance plan. Continually check in and adjust your self-care system accordingly, keeping in mind these key concepts:

Don't forget to share your self-care goals with the #ChooseSelfcare community or you can list them here.

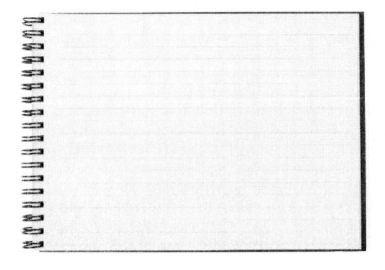

Step 2:

Manage Stress

Chapter 3:
Self-Love Prescription

A physician once said, "The best medicine for humans is love." Someone asked, "What if it doesn't work?" He smiled and said, "Increase the dose." –author unknown

Loving ourselves enough to implement self-care is the beginning. Our perception, and expression, of self-worth is at the core of our mental, physical and emotional wellbeing. It is the foundation to our health and wellness. We often measure self-worth by our level of productivity, hence our perceived value becomes entangled with how busy we appear to be.

This reasoning negatively affects most areas of our lives, including our sleep. The perpetual pursuit of keeping busy leads to rushing around and making hasty lifestyle choices. We subject ourselves, and our families, to harmful fast food, instead of enjoying a thoughtfully prepared meal at the dinner table. This leads not only to inadequate nutrition, but also to poor personal relationships. Wildly shoveling food into our mouths, without mindfully chewing, can also lead to high stress levels and digestive issues. The ripple effect of the busy-life mentality leads us to a deficiency in peace, sustenance, and time—for self-love—or anything else of real value.

Self-Care Check-In

How busy are you? Do you measure your self-worth with productivity? What does your life look like when you are not busy or rushed? Which emotions does that image bring up?

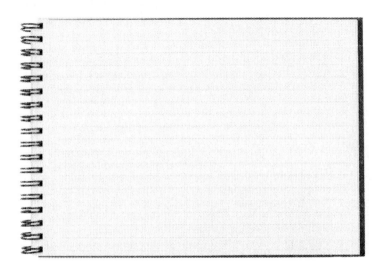

Sleep is an Act of Self-Love

Getting enough sleep (recommended seven to ten hours) has an essential impact on our mood, and our immune system. Unfortunately, when we are feeling out of balance, sleep can be hard to come by. A great way to regain our sense of harmony is to spend time outside, in natural light, and connect with nature by "Earthing." Take your shoes off and connect your bare feet with the earth. By hanging out in nature, and limiting electronic stimulation, you help to rebalance your nervous system and reset the quality of your sleep.

In the winter months, many of us don't receive enough natural light, which can put a slump in our mood. Accordingly, some people are experiencing "seasonal affective disorder." It feels like living with depression half of the year, and impacts emotional *and* physical wellbeing. Installing special, balanced, full spectrum lights inside your home or office can ward off the seasonal blues.

Stress Triggers

Self-care isn't only about nurturing our body. It also encompasses caring for our emotional health. Emotions are intimately linked with our physical wellbeing. Your body's responses to anger or fear are a great example. When the body experiences anger, the blood pressure spikes. When we are fearful, the body produces specific hormones which protect us in the immediate situation. In both cases, the stress-related response may help in the moment, but have long-term damaging effects when they don't automatically ramp back down. If you have other extenuating issues, emotional triggers like these might bring about more complications.

Paying attention to your emotional triggers and reactions can help you to manage your stress levels more effectively. It is helpful to develop a baseline and self-gauging system for your emotional responses. Useful insight can be gathered with the responses to questions like, "Am I able to smile or laugh right now?" Then consider, "If I'm not able to bring on a smile, then I may have high levels of stress—so how is that stress manifesting in my body right now?"

Fortunately, there are plenty of tools available for addressing emotions and mood. The use of essential oils (which we will discuss in the next chapter) can help manage moods in an effective way thereby controlling stress, improving concentration and focus, and remaining calm during the inevitable chaotic times.

Remember, we need to incorporate what we've learned about our strengths and weaknesses from the Self-Care Check-In exercises. In this way we can implement better emotional and physical coping strategies as life throws curve balls or we take on too much. Awareness becomes our most important tool for regaining control of our health and self-care.

Sleep

Getting enough zzzzzz's can have a great impact on not only our mood, but also our health. It is recommended that most people need between seven to ten hours of sleep per night. Limiting caffeine, alcohol and sugar consumption and getting proper nutrition during the day can decrease insomnia and create an environment for adequate rest. There are additional techniques discussed in future chapters to help with many common sleep issues. The important point here is that having sufficient sleep will reduce feelings of stress and anxiety. Those stress triggers may not be quite as overpowering as well if you have had plenty of rest.

Healing Touch

Ayurveda is a health and healing system that emphasizes the prevention of disease, instead of the "wait until something goes wrong" approach our culture tends to practice. A powerful Ayurvedic technique called self-massage is a simple wellness therapy you can do for yourself. This approach is known in Sanskrit as Snehana, or oiling. It translates into "loving your own body." Self-massage is self-love. It communicates a sense of value and worthiness to the body. Developing a strong expression of self-love is crucial for our self-care. It is the foundation for achieving our finest health and wellness.

Here are a few of the great reasons to practice this stress-relieving and mood enhancing therapy:

- Relieves pain
- Improves sleep
- Softens skin
- Calms nerves
- Increases circulation
- Lubricates joints
- Boosts immune system
- Assists with detoxification
- Stimulates digestion
- Tones muscles and tissues
- Decreases signs of aging

Instructions to perform self-massage:

1) You will need warm oil (coconut, sunflower, jojoba, olive, neem, safflower, or almond oil are all good choices). Place your oil of choice into a sealed glass container (mason jars work effectively). Then place the container in a bowl of hot water for several minutes, making sure the oil is warm, but not too hot. You can add essential oils to this base if you'd like (ylang ylang and frankincense essential oils are my personal favorites).
2) Pour a small amount of oil into your palm and begin to massage your head and scalp. I love this—having my hair washed and scalp rubbed is my favorite part of a hair salon visit.
3) Working at a slow pace, move down the neck massaging all sides and include the ears. Remember to keep your breath deep and even.

4) Apply a light layer of oil to the face. Massage upward along the jawline, toward the temples, and back down along the jawbone to the chin. Massage around the eyes and use a circular motion at each temple. Gently tap your fingers along the eyebrow line.

5) Add a liberal amount of oil to the palms. Massage between the fingers, along the back of the hands, over the finger joints, and into your wrists in a circular motion.

6) Apply more oil to your palms as you massage the arms in long sweeping strokes, moving upward toward the heart. Massage the elbow and shoulder joints in circular motions.

7) Apply oil to the chest and abdomen. Gently massage in a clockwise direction. Again, maintain an awareness of your deep, even and controlled breath as you move.

8) Massage the legs in an upward motion using long strokes toward the heart, flowing around the knee and hip joints in a circular motion.

9) Apply oil to the tops and bottoms of the feet, working the oil in-between the toes. Massage the joints, ankles, and heels with a gentle circular motion.

10) Relax and let the oil absorb for about 10 minutes, which provides you with the perfect time to enjoy a cup of tea or warm lemon water. Then rinse off in the shower allowing a light layer of oil to remain on your skin.

Our thoughts about self are vital to our self-care. Negative thoughts can literally grow disease within the body, while positive thinking and self-talk can promote powerful healing.

The Power of Affirmations

If the words we spoke to ourselves appeared on our skin, would we still be beautiful? Self-inflicted attacks happen frequently and can spiral out of control if we don't practice continuous self-love.

Saying positive affirmations during moments of anxiety, self-doubt or panic can provide emotional support. It might seem a little odd, talking to yourself at first, but it becomes more comfortable as you practice. Repeating positive statements about yourself is one of the most effective acts of self-love. It puts a stop to negative self-talk, and can create a sense of peace and hope, diminishing most stressful situations. The key is talking to yourself like you would to someone you love.

Here are a few examples:

- **I am supported, loved and appreciated.**
- **Today is a new day and I will not think about the past or the future. I will be present and enjoy what today has to offer.**
- **I alone am enough. I have nothing to prove to anyone.**

There are lots of available resources to find affirmations, but for the journal exercise below, please use the first ones that come to mind. After you write a few down with today's date, you can come back later and write new ones. This can demonstrate your progress with this program.

Self-Care Check-In

Write a few positive affirmations that you can say about yourself, along with today's date. If this feels uncomfortable, explore why it is uncomfortable. In order to remove what's blocking us, we must confront our fear.

It may take a bit of practice, but with time and gentle effort you will adjust your mental habits away from negative, condemning thoughts about self. In their place will naturally flow these affirmations and positive self-images. You really cannot overdo this – the more positivity you generate toward yourself, the more wonderful and uplifted you will feel. I am certain that other people around you will notice the change as well!

Now that you are feeling more calm, peaceful and loved, let's look at what we've covered. In this chapter, we discussed several new methods you can add to your Self-Care S.Y.S.T.E.M. to manage stress levels. Here are a few of the key concepts discussed, along with a few additional ideas to consider.

Self-Care S.Y.S.T.E.M.

- Untangle your life. Being busy does not increase your value.
- Self-massage promotes healing and sends loving, caring signals to the body.
- Saying positive affirmations can lift mood and minimize anxiety levels.

Remember to share your self-love ideas with #ChooseSelfcare community!

Chapter 4:
Emotional Self-Care with Aromatherapy

Before we discuss how food and mood are connected, we first need to highlight a few tools to help with our current state of emotional health. This is important if you are carrying feelings of doubt, are deficient in self-worth, or are struggling with sadness. When experiencing a negative emotional state, you will most likely lack the motivation to incorporate the subtle changes introduced in the next few chapters. This is where the power of essential oils (EOs) can provide comfort and relief.

Many people have issues with self-worth. We are taught not to be selfish and as we grow up. We confused selfishness with self-worth.

What are Essential Oils?

To define what essential oils (EOs) are all about, I will first need to explain a little science. I promise I won't make you repeat chemistry class. I will instead provide a quick, simple overview on how essential oils work for your body's benefit. This time, the odds really are ever in your favor.

If you have ever enjoyed the sweet scent of a rose, then you have experienced the aromatic qualities of essential oils. These naturally-occurring, aromatic compounds are found in the seeds, bark, stems, roots, flowers, and other parts of plants. Essential oils provide plants with protection against predators and disease, and play a role in plant pollination. In addition to their natural benefits to plants and being beautifully fragrant to people, essential oils have long been used for food preparation, beauty treatments, and healthcare practices. Essential oils present a powerful opportunity to support your body in the amazing healing it does daily, on its own.

Essential Oils
- Natural Aromatic Compounds Found in Plants
- Steam Distilled or Cold Pressed Extraction
- Powerful and Safe Benefits, Without Harmful Side Effects of Medications

My family discovered the power of essential oils when I was seeking a natural solution for our respiratory health and immune function challenges. Over the years, I had suffered from reoccurring sinus infections, and the only solutions my doctors provided were antibiotics (which caused most of my health problems in the first place), steroids, and even highly addictive nose sprays. The addiction to over-the-counter nose sprays became so bad that I was constantly using them and had them stashed all over the house. When I found I needed a nose spray upstairs, another downstairs, one in my purse, and another in each of our cars, it became clear—I needed to find a better solution.

I soon discovered essential oils. I began seeing improvements when I used lavender, lemon, and peppermint essential oils to address environmental threats, and eucalyptus oil for clearing the respiratory tract. Finally, I had no more congestion. I could breathe without reaching for a nose spray. Once I saw how well essential oils worked for me in this way, it sparked my desire to learn how I could use them throughout our home.

Essential oils do not cure or heal.
Essential oils only provide the body with what it needs in order for the body to heal itself.

Essential oils are very potent and concentrated. Not all essential oils are created equal though. In fact, it is important to note that many suppliers do not verify the purity of the oils they distribute.[3] There is currently no committee or governing body that regulates essential oils, their purity, or the claims made by many essential oil companies. It is important to choose your oils carefully. Rather than search for bargains, look for quality, instead.

There are three different types of essential oils: Synthetic, Food Grade, and Therapeutic. Synthetic essential oils are used in the manufacturing of air fresheners and scented candles. The scent of the products is pleasant, but there are no therapeutic benefits to be gained from synthetic essential oils.

One step up from synthetic EOs are food grade essential oils. These are used in flavoring toothpaste and gum. The US Food and Drug Administration has approved these oils to be used in food preparation, but again, there are no therapeutic benefits to these oils. They are used solely to enhance flavoring of products.

The premium category of oils is the 100% therapeutic-grade essential oils. These have been used throughout history for the health benefits they are able to deliver.

It is crucial that you use only pure, therapeutic grade essential oils sourced from the plants' native region—its natural environment. For both the plants and oils inside, that's where the magic happens. While many plants can be, and are, grown all around the world, certain plants thrive in specific areas of the globe. Only plants grown in these optimum areas produce the premier oils needed for the most effective healing.

As an example, while lavender could be grown in Kentucky, the French climate and environmental conditions are one of the most ideal for premium lavender. This perfect blend of environment and climate infuse the plants, and thus the extracted essential oils are of higher quality and are more effective in delivering their benefits.

There are three ways to experience essential oils, but in this chapter, we will only focus on using essential oils aromatically and topically and their associated emotional self-care benefits.

Aromatically:
- Affects mood
- Cleanses the air
- Open airways

Topically:
- Works fast, entering the blood stream in about 30 seconds
- Systemic, from whole body to localized effects
- Massage
- Immediate comfort
- Immune support

Internally:
- Detoxifies the body
- Supports the digestive system

One of the most dynamic ways to experience essential oils is through simple inhalation. The inhalation of essential oils is a powerful method to affect memory, hormones, brain function, and emotional health through the olfactory system. When we inhale air through the nose, it passes over the olfactory membranes. At this point chemicals suspended in that air stimulate the olfactory receptor cells.
This information then moves from the receptor-cell neurons to the first cranial nerve and on to the frontal lobes of the brain.
Our mind generates powerful neural connections between scent and emotions. Diffusing essential oils into the air and breathing them in is a simple yet effective way to access those connections. Engaging with

essential oils in this way can also help develop correlations between new memories and experiences.

Essential Oil Demonstration: Aromatic

Scientists have identified about 350 separate olfactory receptors in the human nose while discovering 150 or so, of these receptors in other organs, including the heart and liver.[5]

To experience what essential oil aromatherapy can offer, simply open a bottle of peppermint essential oil and inhale, or put a few drops of oil on the palm of your hand and rub your hands together. Cupping your hands over your nose and mouth, inhale a few times while carefully avoiding your eyes.* You can even add a few drops of oil to a bowl of hot (not boiling) water and inhale the vapor that rises from the bowl.

Take note: if you get an essential oil in your eyes, instead of rinsing with water, flush it out with a carrier oil such as coconut oil or olive oil.

You should feel the effects of the oil entering your nose and igniting the sensors in your body. The single drop of peppermint oil, if it is a true 100% pure, thera-peutic-grade oil, would be about as strong as 25 cups of peppermint herbal tea. It should help energize you while simultaneously clearing your respiratory tract.

Because cold-air diffusion distributes essential oil molecules into the air so effectively, it is an excellent way to maximize the beneficial properties of essential oils. When inhaling an essential oil, its molecules can reach the brain within 22 seconds, making it a powerful resource for emotional self-care. There are lots of different ways to diffuse, but it is important to note that overheating essential oils using aroma lamps or candles can diminish some of the beneficial properties of the essential oils. Stay with either direct inhalation or cold-air diffusers when you are using essential oils.

Getting Started with Topical Use: Neat vs. Carrier Oil
When applied topically (to the skin), essential oils are easily absorbed and quickly enter the bloodstream. This is one reason why the quality of the oil is so important. Many high-quality oils are safe to use *neat*, which means applied directly to the skin without combining with a carrier oil. It is always a good idea to test a small sample on your skin to determine if you have any particular sensitivity or reaction.

A *carrier oil* is a base oil used to dilute essential oils. They are referred to as carrier oils because they help carry the essential oil safely into the skin, and stop the essential oil from evaporating too quickly. A carrier oil that I frequently use is fractionated coconut oil, which is solid coconut oil with a triglyceride naturally removed so the oil remains constantly liquid at room temperature. This formulation makes creating roller blends easier when the coconut oil remains in liquid form.

Carrier Oils:
Coconut oil/fractionated coconut oil, olive oil, grape seed oil, avocado oil, almond oil, apricot oil, jojoba oil, castor oil

(The easiest and safest place to topically apply essential oils is to the soles of the feet) There are two places you never want to use essential oils: in the ears and in the eyes. I can't remind you enough, if you get an essential oil in your eye (*ouch*), do not use water (remember oil and water don't mix) but instead use a carrier oil to flush it out.

When using essential oils topically, you should note that some essential oils are photosensitive (mainly the citrus oils). You will want to avoid using them on skin that will be directly exposed to sunlight, otherwise you might receive an unexpected sunburn.

If you are concerned with how much essential oil to use, remember—less is always better. The appropriate dosage for topical use of essential oils is different for each individual as well as for each oil. A plan for essential oils should be customized for the person's distinct circumstances and characteristics. Here is a recommended dilution ratio for topical use.

Dilution Chart

	0.5%	1.0%	2.0%	3.0%	10%	25%
5 ml (1 tsp)		1 drop	2 drops	3 drops	10 drops	25 drops
10 ml (2 tsp)	1 drop	2 drops	4 drops	6 drops	20 drops	50 drops
15 ml (1/2 oz)	1.5 drops	3 drops	6 drops	9 drops	30 drops	75 drops
30 ml (1 oz)	3 drops	6 drops	12 drops	18 drops	60 drops	150 drops

Limbic System

The limbic system is a complex system of nerves within the brain that control mood and basic emotions. Some of these emotions are fear, pleasure and anger. Being able to manage our emotions can help manage our stress levels.

Because smells are delivered directly to the brain, where our limbic system evaluates the stimuli, they serve as emotional triggers. This is a key factor as to why essential oils are successful assisting our emotional self-care. Essential oils can facilitate a quick emotional response in the brain, which helps us to direct our own emotional traffic.[5]

Introduction to Individual Essential Oils

Bergamot essential oil is great for attending to the symptoms of depression because it is very stimulating. This essential oil can create feelings of joy, freshness and energy by improving the blood circulation. A study done in 2011 found that Bergamot lowered the anxiety response, making it an effective natural remedy for anxiety.[6] Try diffusing Bergamot or rubbing it on your feet or chest.

Inhaling **Ylang Ylang** essential oil can deliver immediate, positive effects on the mood. Research has shown it can even help release negative emotions such as anger, low self-esteem, and even jealousy.[7] To enhance confidence, mood, and self-love, try diffusing Ylang Ylang or massaging it into your skin. I keep Ylang Ylang in a roller bottle inside my purse and roll it onto my wrists as a nice replacement for synthetic perfumes.

Diffusing **Lavender** essential oil near your bed while you sleep will improve restfulness. Additionally, rubbing this oil behind your ears can relieve stress and lower anxiety levels. Several studies have proven lavender's benefits to address anxiety and poor mood without any harmful side effects.[8]
The results of another study revealed that lavender oil, when used daily, helped decrease depression by 32.7 percent and dramatically decreased sleep disturbances, moodiness and overall health in 47 people suffering from PTSD.[9]

Roman Chamomile has been rated as one of the best medicinal herbs for fighting stress and promoting relaxation. According to published research, inhaling roman chamomile is good for maintaining emotional balance and as a natural remedy for anxiety and general depression.[10]

Calming Essential Oils	Results
Lavender Geranium Patchouli Melissa Vetiver Sandalwood Ylang Ylang Jasmine Clary Sage Tangerine Roman Chamomile Marjoram	Encourages a restful state for mind and body Reduces Stress & Anxiety

Uplifting Essential Oils	Results
Bergamot Melissa Grapefruit Sandalwood Lemongrass Tangerine Lemon Ylang Ylang Cedarwood Clary Sage Peppermint Wild Orange	Promotes a cheerful, positive attitude

After reviewing the two categories above, you might notice that some of the essential oils overlap. How can that happen? Earlier we discussed the strong connection between smell and memories. One person can smell Ylang Ylang and remember a time that triggers them to relax and calm their mental state, while another person can smell Ylang Ylang and feel uplifted and reassured. Often, it is the trigger that is the key, so you might revisit our analysis of triggers from Chapter 2 as you experiment with essential oils.

Essential Oil Blends to Get You Started

Lemon essential oil is invigorating and uplifting. It promotes physical energy and purification. For an attitude adjustment, diffuse lemon essential oil throughout your day to promote a brighter perspective when you are feeling down. Below are several different essential oil blends that use this uplifting, vibrant oil. These can be diffused or applied topically to the back of the neck or wrist.

Happy Morning Blend:
1 drop Peppermint, 1 drop Wild Orange, 1 drop Lemon

Focus Facilitator Blend:
2 drops Lemon and 2 drops Frankincense

Citrus Smiles Blend:
1 drop Lemon, 1 drop Wild Orange, 1 drop Grapefruit

Refresh & Revive Blend:
2 drops Lemon and 2 drops Eucalyptus oil

Mood Management Blend:
2 drops Lemon and 3 drops Geranium essential oil

Energy Trio:
1 drop Rosemary, 1 drop Peppermint, 1 drop Lemon

Oils and Blends for Specific Symptoms
Brain Fog - Feelings of mental confusion or lack of mental clarity

- Arborvitae
- Eucalyptus
- Douglas Fir
- Juniper Berry
- Frankincense
- Peppermint
- Lemon
- Lime
- Lavender

Focus & Attention Essential Oil Blend:
5 drops Peppermint, 5 drops Wild Orange, 2 drops Frankincense
     Add to diffuser and ENJOY!

Fatigue
- Basil
- Cassia
- Cinnamon
- Coriander
- Lemon
- Thyme
- Ginger

Uplift Roller-bottle Blend: (Elevate and Inspire)
- Inspire a shift towards action
- Elevate mood towards positive thinking
10 drops Peppermint, 5 drops Roman Chamomile, 10 drops Wild Orange, 2 drops Frankincense
     Place drops in a 1-ounce roller-bottle, fill remainder with carrier oil.

Nervous Fatigue
- Rosemary

Stress Reliever Blend:
4 drops Wild Orange, 2 drops Frankincense

Mental Fatigue
- Basil
- Lemongrass
- Grapefruit

Focus/Energy Blend:
3 drops Peppermint, 3 drops Wild Orange

Insomnia - feelings of sleeplessness
- Vetiver
- Lavender

Good Night Sleep Blend:
3 drops Cedarwood, 5 drops Lavender

Sweet Dreams Blend:
1 drop Juniper Berry, 1 drop Roman Chamomile, 1 drop Lavender

Sleep Well Diffuser Blend:
3 drops Vetiver, 3 drops Lavender, 3 drops Sandalwood, 3 drops Cedarwood

Stress and Anxiety
Apply 1 drop Peppermint and 1 drop Lavender essential oils to the neck and forehead to relieve tension and pressure.

Encouragement Blend: (Motivate, Invigorate, & Stimulate)
- Promotes feelings of confidence, courage, & belief.
- Counteracts negative emotions of doubt, pessimism and cynicism.

4 drops Peppermint, 4 drops Clementine, 3 drops Coriander, 4 drops Basil, 4 drops Melissa, 3 drops Rosemary

Self-Worth
Place 1-2 drops Grapefruit essential oil topically to the chest or diffuse to encourage positive relationships with yourself and decrease negative self-talk.

Love Yourself Blend:
1 drop Sandalwood, 1 drop Geranium, 1 drop Wild Orange, 1 drop Bergamot, 1 drop Ylang Ylang

Feelings of Fear:
- Myrrh
- Juniper Berry
- Frankincense

Mellow Out Blend:
10 drops Lavender, 10 drops Wild Orange, 2 drops of Marjoram, 2 drops Frankincense
Mix in a 10ml roller-bottle and top off with fractionated coconut oil. Apply behind ears, to the soles of the feet or down the spine.

Self-Care Check-In

How can using essential oils benefit your self-care S.Y.S.T.E.M.? Which oils or blends are you drawn toward the most?

Self-Care S.Y.S.T.E.M.

- Use high-quality, pure, therapeutic-grade essential oils.
- Essential oils are very potent and concentrated.
- Never use essential oils in the eyes or ears.
- Dilute with a carrier oil and not water (remember oil and water don't mix).
- Avoid using photosensitive oils on skin directly exposed to sunlight.
- Essential oils are effective without the harmful side effects that come with synthetic prescription medications.

Share your favorite blends with the #ChooseSelfcare community

Step 3:

Reduce Toxic Load

Chapter 5:
Fake Food in a Real World

Every day we encounter toxins in the air we breathe, things we touch, and food we eat. The goal is to minimize our exposure to these toxins so our bodies can thrive, and not be pushed into illness from toxic overload. Consistent detoxification is crucial in our modern world full of daily contact with chemicals.

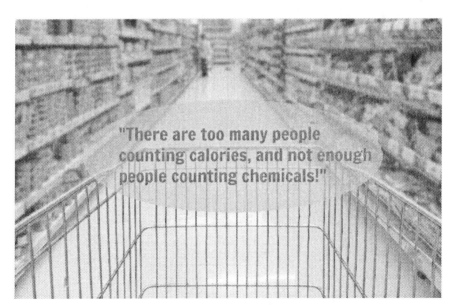

"There are too many people counting calories, and not enough people counting chemicals!"

Importance of Detoxification

Detoxification describes the process of eliminating unwanted substances from the body. Releasing toxins allows the body to dedicate more energy to thriving rather than just coping with difficulty. When a person is overwhelmed by toxins, their bodily functions cannot perform properly. Metabolism, immunity, nutrient absorption, brain function, reproduction, respiration, and even circulation are all affected.

"People are fed by the food industry which pays no attention to health, and are treated by the health industry, which pays no attention to food." – Wendell Berry[11]

Even our drinking water has become processed. The chemicals added to our tap water have caused more health problems than they were designed to address. Having access to water that is free from contaminants, such as fluoride, is an essential component of regaining health and reducing inflammatory response in the body.

It's time to reframe our perceptions when it comes to the chemicals and potential toxins that are all around us—particularly the ones we ingest, both knowingly and unknowingly. Many of these substances that seem innocuous enough, can have huge negative impacts on our health, mood and overall wellbeing. Let's start by cutting the "CRAP" and replacing it with "FOOD."

C-arbonated Drinks
R-efined Sugar
A-rtificial Sweeteners/Colors
P-rocessed Foods

F-ruit and Vegetables
O-rganic Lean Protein
O-mega 3 Fatty Acids
D-rink Water

When Life Gives You Lemons, Drink Lemon Water

Not sure where to start on your detox journey? Choose lemon water. Lemon juice is great at detoxing. Add a tablespoon of lemon juice to a glass of water and drink it. This will assist in deep cleansing of the liver and kidneys from toxic overload that may be causing inflammation within the body. If having fresh lemons is difficult, stock up on organic lemons (great during a sale) and squeeze all of them. Place the juice in ice cube trays and freeze. One cube is just right for a glass of water. You now have them readily available anytime to throw into water or a smoothie.

Ayurvedic Lemon Technique

Drinking warm lemon water on an empty stomach about 30 minutes before eating is an ancient Ayurvedic method used to cleanse the body. The additional benefits of this practice include improved digestion, bolstering the immune system, alkalizing the body, reducing mucus and phlegm production, aiding in weight loss efforts and decreasing appearance of acne. Here is a quick concoction you can easily prepare first thing in the morning:

Morning Detox Recipe

1 tablespoon organic apple cider vinegar
1 teaspoon raw honey
1 tablespoon lemon juice
1 teaspoon ginger
1 teaspoon cinnamon
10 ounces warm water
Combine and drink

Kick the Caffeine Habit

When we start to assess the chemicals we are ingesting on a daily basis, a few of them jump to the forefront. Many of us cannot even start our day until we get a bit of one particular chemical into our bloodstream – caffeine. I'll admit, it's a pretty nice feeling to grab that steaming mug of coffee first thing on a chilly morning, but there are definitely biological repercussions we need to be aware of when we make that decision.

Coffee affects the sympathetic nervous system, leading to many health concerns which can end up triggering anxiety and sleep disorders. Research links caffeine to the suppression of serotonin production in the body.[12] Caffeine in coffee also gives a diuretic effect, so you will start to feel dehydrated quickly. In addition, because you are drinking coffee in the morning, you are probably having that instead of water.

When you wake up, you are already a bit dehydrated from your sleep cycle, then you are dehydrating yourself even more and not replenishing your body.

Essential Oil for Caffeine Replacement

Peppermint essential oil will help wake you up naturally without the cups of coffee. Place 1 drop of peppermint oil into your palm and rub your hands together. Next cup your hands over your nose and mouth (making sure to avoid your eyes) and inhale deeply through your nose to increase alertness and focus. You can also reach for rosemary essential oil when studying for a test, instead of reaching for a caffeinated drink. Diffuse it to boost your concentration and focus.

Fortunately, there are some good alternatives available in the market for you now. If you can't give up the coffee taste, try Teeccino. They have a large selection of herbal coffees without caffeine, and without those side effects. Of course, choosing tea is a good way to reduce caffeine consumption and help you taper off in a more gentle way.

When it comes to caffeine, there is another major culprit that is usually prominent in our diet—caffeinated sodas. These bad boys are highly addictive with loads of sugar and chemicals. I should know—I was a *soda junkie*. There were days I would drink 5-9 cans of soda to get me through a work day. One of the ways I ditched the soda was decreasing the amount slowly each week and drinking more sparkling waters. Sometimes the bubbles of the sparkling water would help with the soda fix, until I eventually phased them out completely. Infusing waters with fruits and vegetables will help take the boring out if the water, and make it more fun.

Win the Battle Over Smoking

Obviously, smoking is a habit that needs to be considered when doing a detox. I probably don't need to tell you that the damage to physical health is enormous. However, those who smoke still do so out of habit and addiction. Many people eliminated smoking by using the nicotine patch system. That is one solution. Essential oils are an additional technique to ease discomfort while phasing out tobacco products. Keep focusing on how good you will feel after you have kicked the "S" habit—and how much money you'll save by not buying cigarettes.

Quit Sticks

Black pepper and cinnamon essential oils inhalation can drastically help reduced cigarette cravings. Pour 2 tsp. of fractionated coconut oil in an 8 oz. mason jar. Add 15 drops each of cinnamon and black pepper essential oils. Arrange toothpicks standing up in the jar so all are touching the oil on the bottom. Put the lid on the jar and allow it to stand until the toothpicks soak up all the oil. Use a toothpick before the cravings hit!

Share your quit smoking victories at #ChooseSelfcare.

Mini Pantry Makeover

Another step in the cleansing process is what I like to call a pantry makeover. Usually I go to a client's home (or if they are not local, work with them through a video Skype call) during a pantry makeover. Since this is a mini pantry makeover, I have listed the culprits to spot and remove below. This will be easier than it might sound at first glance.

Go to your kitchen pantry or wherever you keep the non-refrigerated foods. Start by snapping a photo. You can do the same with your fridge and freezer. You will want to have a nice visual of where you started. It may not seem shocking now, but it will once you revisit them later.

Next, look at every label and set aside all food items that contain the six scary ingredients below.

Use the #ChooseSelfcare to post pictures of your before- and after- pantry makeovers.

Check Your Labels — The Scary Six:
1) Residue – pesticides, herbicides, antibiotics, steroids
2) Flavorings – MSG, natural flavorings
3) Additives – thickening agents, artificial flavors, colors, fillers
4) Bad fats – hydrogenated oils
5) Sweet Stuff – artificial sweeteners and real sugar
6) GMOs- more residue

Opt for Organic

There has long been a debate over the nutritional benefits of organic versus conventional foods. Also argued is whether the pesticides absorbed by conventional produce causes harm to those who consume it. Each day, there are more studies to support that eating organic food is better for our health. There are plenty of studies linking the use of pesticides to neurological disorders.

Organic foods offer at least one undisputed advantage— significantly fewer harmful pesticides and herbicides, which minimizes your exposure to cell-damaging toxic chemicals. Reducing your exposure to pesticides can increase immunity and decrease allergies. It may also support weight loss and fertility. Start by buying organics for the worst pesticide offenders.

It should be easy to find a list of the ones you should focus on, but there are also some common-sense tips you can leverage when making decisions. Produce with thin, porous skin enable easy transfer of chemicals like pesticides through into the entirety of the fruit or vegetable. Examples here would be apples and grapes. In addition, we normally ingest the skins or coverings of these foods (and in the case of the non-organic varieties, the pesticides that have congregated on them as well).

Conversely, foods that are a bit more resistant to the penetration of pesticides are those with harder and less porous coverings. Think of the hard rinds of pineapples, cantaloupes and avocadoes as excellent examples. We cannot digest those skins, and it is quite difficult for pesticides to get inside as well. You might also consider swapping out conventional dairy products, where pesticides tend to concentrate rather easily.

Since many grocery stores are limited in their organic produce options, you may need to utilize a bit of this logic as you make your shopping decisions. But remember, these suggestions are simply guides for you to make better choices. They are not intended to stress you out when you have only non-organic options available. This is a "Self-Care Guide," not a "Beat You Up For Not Eating Perfectly Guide." If you are consumed with stress when shopping at the grocery store, just breathe and remember to make the best choices you can, in the moment.

A better option would to be to grow your own produce, but for many this is not possible. If you are in an apartment or have only a small yard, you could grow herbs or a few leafy greens in a window container. You might be able to get permission to maintain a raised garden in your courtyard or a park. You could research what buying or co-op options might be available to you.

Additionally, you could get to know the nearby farmers and attend local farmers' markets. A lot of times the prices on produce and other items such as eggs are much less expensive when you deal directly with the farmer. There is no middle man (a.k.a. the grocery store), to mark up prices, and you have fresher options available to you. It's a Win-Win.

Don't forget to thoroughly wash your produce before preparing to eat. Also make a note to wash produce even if you do not intend to eat the outside skin, such as a lemon. When you cut open a lemon, if you did not properly wash the outside of it, you could be contaminating the knife and the inside part of the lemon, as the blade cuts through. It is better to be safe than sorry, so wash everything.

Another option is to rinse or soak your fruits and vegetables with vinegar or essential oils. This can have a huge impact on how long they last, and has the added benefit of removing the waxy film from them. A study published in 2003 in the "Journal of Food Protection" found that washing apples with a vinegar and water solution reduced salmonella on the outer skin significantly more than washing with water alone.[13]

Fruit & Veggie Wash
Soak your produce for a few minutes in the sink with a mixture of the ratio 1 cup vinegar to 5 cups of filtered water. You can rub while you rinse. This will

remove wax, pesticides, and dirt. If you don't want to go the vinegar route, you can put 2-5 drops of therapeutic-grade lemon essential oil into your filtered water and stir the produce around making sure it comes into contact with the oil.

Clean Cooking

Switching to stainless, cast iron, glass, or non-toxic ceramic cookware will provide a clean and safe start to your cooking process. Plastics and non-stick Teflon can leach hormone disrupting chemicals into your food. That is no good when you just put effort into cooking a nice meal.

Take caution with non-stick cooking sprays, as they can contain heavily processed chemicals, which are often linked to disease. Additionally, being aware of the smoke point for your cooking oils is quite often overlooked. Some oils, such as olive oil do not have a high smoke point. If used in high heat cooking, the oil can turn toxic and cause inflammation within your body. Pay attention to labels to avoid unhealthy oils such as vegetable and canola oil. A great alternative for a cooking oil with a high smoke point is ghee. It is a type of clarified butter and is a significantly healthier option.

Natural Cleaning Solutions

Another way to detox your body, and your home, is to switch from chemically-infused synthetic cleaning products to essential oils. As we discussed in the previous chapter, there are several additional health benefits to essential oils. There are two main oils that my family uses in our home. Lavender essential oil is antiseptic as well as being a great cleaning oil. Use it in a spray for tabletops or in water to mop the floor. Lemon essential oil is a natural disinfectant. It will cleanse an area of bacteria, germs and other contaminants.

Non Toxic Cleaners

Natural Air Freshener
Put ¼ cup baking soda into a small Mason jar. Add 5-6 drops of your favorite essential oil or blend. Cover top with a piece of fabric, securing it with a rubber band or the metal band part of the lid.

Carpet Freshener
Pour a box of baking soda into a container with a cover that has holes poked in the top. Add 20 drops of your favorite essential oil and shake. Sprinkle over your carpet and let set for 15 minutes before vacuuming.

Disinfecting Window/Surface Cleaner
Add 1 drop each of wild orange, clove, cinnamon, eucalyptus, and rosemary essential oils to 1 cup of white vinegar and 1 cup of filtered water into a spray bottle.

Floor Cleaner
Add 3 to 5 drops of lavender, melaleuca (also known as tea tree) essential oil to your mop bucket with water. These oils will help you disinfect your floors.

Natural Beauty Solutions

Since our skin is our largest organ, and whatever we put on it is absorbed into our bloodstream, it makes perfect sense to use chemical-free beauty products. Replace chemically-altered lotions with a carrier oil (coconut, olive, jojoba are all wonderful selections), and add your choice of essential oils for a nice scent and therapeutic benefits. Massage gently into skin for its anti-aging and skin-healing qualities.

Dry Brushing

Dry brushing is a simple way to unclog pores, stimulate circulation and promote detoxing within the body. It is great for the lymphatic system. Take a natural (not synthetic) brush with a long handle. Begin brushing by starting at your feet in long sweeping motions toward your heart. Always brush toward your heart. Once you have brushed your entire body a few times, jump in a hot shower to rinse off and stimulate blood circulation.

Non Toxic Beauty

Perfume- Make Your Own Blend
Or try this one...Romantic Garden Blend:
Mix with 2 tablespoons of vodka or water:
20 drops orange essential oil
5 drops lavender essential oil
10 drops patchouli essential oil
10 drops cedarwood essential oil
5 drops ylang ylang essential oil
5 drops bergamot essential oil

Bath Salts

Mix Epsom salts and lavender, roman chamomile, or ylang ylang essential oils and pour into your warm bath to enjoy!

✳ *Eyelash Lengthener*
Add a drop of therapeutic-grade lavender essential oil or rosemary essential oil to your

favorite non-toxic mascara. The oil helps promote your eyelash growth and strength.

✳ *Soothing Body Lotion*
Add one drop of therapeutic-grade frankincense to 1 tbsp of coconut oil and massage into skin. Your skin will thank you! After too much sun, add one drop each of frankincense, peppermint, and lavender essential oils to your coconut oil for soothing relief.

Homemade Toothpaste
Another often chemical-laden product that we often forget that we are putting into our bodies multiple times every day is toothpaste. Even when we are not fully ingesting it, the synthetic compounds do absorb easily into the gums and even the hard tooth enamel and can cause unintended immune reactions in the body. Here is a wonderful recipe to make a natural toothpaste alternative that will also save you quite a bit of money.

Ingredients
½ cup Coconut oil
2-3 tbsp Baking soda
1 Tbsp Xylitol, blended into a fine powder (plus more to taste)
10 drops Essential oils (peppermint, cinnamon and wild orange)

Instructions
•   Melt the coconut oil on low heat. I use a double-boiler method by putting the coconut oil in the glass jar that I use to store my toothpaste, and then placing the jar into a pan of lightly, simmering water.

- Remove from heat once melted, and stir in baking soda.
- In a blender, blend the xylitol into a fine powder so that it easily dissolves.
- Add the xylitol to the mixture. Feel free to add more if you would like the toothpaste to taste sweeter.
- Add essential oils.
- Once the mixture has solidified, give it another good stir (the baking soda may be settled on the bottom).

Notes
To brush, wet your toothbrush, and dip it in the paste, or scoop a small amount on with a spoon if you want to avoid "double-dipping."

Teeth Whitening
Brush with activated charcoal to naturally whiten teeth.

Homemade Mouth Wash
Mix distilled water with a few drops of melaleuca essential oil to replace your mouth wash.

Minimize Allergens
There may be a few common foods that unknowingly make you sick. Eliminating foods like dairy, wheat, soy, eggs, nuts, and corn, can make a dramatic improvement in your health. It takes several weeks to detox these foods completely out of your system. Once you have done so, you can slowly introduce one back in at a time to see if your body reacts. If a rash, headache or digestive trouble reemerges, you have an allergic reaction to that food type.

The discovery of a food sensitivity can make all the difference in your allergies and health journey. Consider this option of food elimination when detoxing. If your body is working overtime to fight perceived allergens, due either to environment or food, your liver cannot work at its optimal level.

In addition to food sensitivities, many people are also unknowingly suffering from candida overgrowth. We will discuss this significant health challenge in the next chapter. However, for people dealing with candida, any allergies or other sensitivities are frequently intensified greatly. This could lead to overuse of OTC (over-the-counter) medications and possibly to a dependency on those substances.

As I mentioned in an earlier chapter, I suffered severe allergy issues. My doctors were constantly prescribing antibiotics for my frequent sinus infections. It turned into a domino effect, causing bigger health issues which ultimately led to my diagnosis of depression. There are many ways to deal with the symptoms naturally. Here are a few examples:

- Food allergy elimination diet
- Limit exposure to pet dander and other environment or seasonal threats
- Therapeutic-grade essential oils, such as lemon, lavender, and peppermint
- Invest in a Neti pot to clean out nasal passages

Prevention is key. If you don't eat things that were grown in, or coated with pesticides, and minimize your toxic exposures, your liver won't have as much detox work to do.

Self-Care S.Y.S.T.E.M.

- Infrared saunas and lymphatic massage are additional ways to help your body detox.
- Work with a local Food co-op to cut down your organic grocery bill.
- Save money by making your own natural cleaners and non-toxic beauty products using essential oils.
- Explore an elimination diet and journal your findings.

Self-Care Check-In

Which of these detoxification methods resonates the most with you? Take a moment to jot down your thoughts about which actions you can incorporate into your life, body and home.

Share your detoxing journey with the #ChooseSelfcare community

Chapter 6: Candida Epidemic

It is estimated that 80% of Americans have some amount of candida overgrowth[14]. Many of those cases go undiagnosed or are completely misdiagnosed by the modern allopathic healthcare system. This happens because the current paradigm is to treat the symptoms rather than finding the root cause of the original problem. Lack of good nutritional habits, gut health, and stress management are not topics most regular doctors consider when diagnosing their patients. When the problems continue, candida can release toxins into the bloodstream which cause chronic inflammation throughout the body.

To better understand why candida can be such a huge problem, we need to address what it is. "Candida is a yeast, which is a form of fungus, a very small amount of which lives in our mouths and intestines. Its job is to aid with digestion and nutrient absorption, but when overproduced it can cause lots of physical and mental side effects."[15]

Anxiety, depression, irritability, brain fog, poor memory, and lack of concentration are all symptoms that may be attributed to candida overgrowth. When there is an imbalance between candida and helpful bacteria, the candida can mutate and grow rapidly, causing dangerous and painful conditions in the body.

Key factors that increase the risk of candida overgrowth are:

- Lack of friendly bacteria in the GI tract
- Diets high in sugar, high-fructose corn syrup, processed foods, yeast, or alcohol
- Single round of antibiotics or oral contraceptives
- Stress

Life After Antibiotics

Antibiotics have an important role in medical care, but they are being overprescribed. While killing the bad bacteria for which they are prescribed, antibiotics disrupt the natural balance of intestinal flora, or good bacteria that helps ward off disease. This in turn lowers our immune system function and makes us more susceptible to further sickness. It is important for our digestion to have enough good bacteria. This also impacts mood, since the majority of our serotonin is produced in the gut. For these reasons, it makes sense to use more natural solutions, when we can, rather than antibiotics.

Here are a few examples of natural solutions with antibiotic properties:

Manuka Honey – Due to its strong antibiotic properties, it is often used as a topical treatment for minor cuts and scrapes.

Raw Garlic – A powerful antioxidant with antibacterial, antifungal, and antiviral agents.

Echinacea – A well-known cold and flu combatant due to its immune-strengthening and antimicrobial properties. It has been traditionally used among Native Americans to fight many conditions, including blood poisoning, bladder infections, strep throat and even headaches.

Goldenseal – It can be used for prevention of strep throat when 1 teaspoon of powder is gargled with a pinch of salt and hot water.

A persistent sinus or ear infection (a very common sign of yeast overgrowth) can recur after you have finished your antibiotic medication. The symptoms may temporarily disappear but the root problem has not been discovered and addressed. Taking another round of antibiotics for the subsequent infection will only feed the candida, further exacerbating the bacterial imbalance and complicating the symptoms.

The symptoms below can be attributed, in part, to an overgrowth of candida. Check the box next to the ones that you are experiencing. ☑

Candida Symptoms:
(Many are the same as depression symptoms)
- Acne
- Acid Reflux
- Allergies
- Anxiety
- Autoimmune Conditions
- Bloating
- Constipation
- Depression
- Diarrhea
- Ear Infections
- Eczema
- Brain fog
- Chronic Fatigue
- Depression
- Eczema
- Food Cravings: Sugar & Carbs
- Fungal Infections of skin or nails
- Irritable bowel syndrome (IBS)
- Low immune system
- Mood Swings
- Panic attacks
- Psoriasis
- Rash

- Sinus Infections
- Sleep Disturbances
- Sore Muscles
- Thyroid symptoms
- Weight loss resistance or Weight Gain
- Yeast Infections

If you checked off several symptoms and think you might be suffering from candida overgrowth, there are certainly some actions you can immediately take.

What to Do
1) Get a comprehensive blood, urine, and stool test specific for candida
2) Consider lifestyle and diet changes to decrease stress and remove toxins
3) Supplement with strong probiotics and antifungal agents
4) Follow a Candida Cleanse Program

There is no "one-size-fits-all" solution when it comes to overcoming candida. This is why it is important to get the comprehensive tests done in order to see how aggressive your response will need to be in order to fight it off properly.

Systemic yeast infections are linked to the dozens of auto-immune conditions that many people suffer from. Attending to the root cause is essential to developing long-lasting wellness. The growing prevalence of gluten intolerance, which affects the gastrointestinal and nervous systems, is also associated with these types of overgrowths. Candida can suppress thyroid hormones that regulate metabolism and heart rate, and put stress on the adrenal glands. All of these things negatively impact the immune system and the overall energy levels in the body.

We need to bring the infection under control, thereby restoring our energy levels and strengthening our immune systems. How do we do this? We must starve out that pesky yeast by removing all the foods from our diet that encourage its growth, while simultaneously building a balanced gut ecosystem.

The best way to regain control over a systemic yeast infection is to incorporate a diet free of sugar and gluten. The diet should instead contain plentiful amounts of probiotics and alkaline-forming, plant-based foods. The alkalizing effect is absolutely essential here. When you significantly change the pH level of your body, you create unfavorable conditions for the growth of yeast (like candida) and other harmful microorganisms.

How to Control Candida

Getting rid of the candida overgrowth primarily requires you to embrace a low-sugar diet. Sugar feeds yeast and encourages its growth. Eliminating sugar in all of its simple forms is a must. Cut out pasta, bread, baked cookies, muffins, bagels and most (if not all) processed foods. Talk to your healthcare professional about administering a stool test to determine how severe the candida overgrowth is. The methods for getting rid of candida overgrowth range from simple to extreme, and not all plans will be right for you.

Basic Foods to Avoid
- Sugar & Fruit
- Grains
- Dairy (Except Probiotics) & Soy Products
- Caffeine & Alcohol
- Condiments
- Artificial Ingredients/ Preservatives
- Starchy Vegetables
- Processed Meats
- Peanuts, Cashews, Pistachios

- Beans and Mushrooms
- Peanut Oil, Corn Oil, Canola Oil

Top 15 Foods That Fight Candida
- Garlic
- Onions
- Probiotics
- Cinnamon
- Cloves
- Oregano
- Turmeric
- Olive Oil
- Avocado
- Ginger
- Cruciferous vegetables like broccoli & brussels sprouts
- Coconut Oil
- Apple Cider Vinegar
- Lemon Juice

How Long Does the Candida Cleanse Take?
The cleansing process depends on a combination of factors:
- How strictly you adhere to the dietary restrictions and suggestions listed above.
- How severe your candida overgrowth is.
- How aggressively you supplement with probiotics and antifungals.

The balance of these factors will be unique to you. Set aside thoughts of comparison to other people. Those thoughts can be self-sabotaging and lead to feelings of failure.

Most people struggle with eliminating their favorite foods during the cleanse process, which in turn leads them to quit and return to unhealthy habits before they are able experience the benefits. Focus on what you *can* eat rather than what you need to eliminate. This will help with your perspective and make the cleanse process far more tolerable.

If you decide to engage in a candida cleanse, it is good to be prepared for the emotional upheaval that usually presents itself during the first few weeks of the plan. When candida die-off occurs, it causes some physical discomfort and strong emotions often bubble up to the surface. This is completely normal and if you stay strong and get through the initial die-off period, you will experience the benefits—*believe me.*

I went through severe joint pain and melodramatic crying fits when I undertook my candida cleanse several years ago. After a week, my entire world began to shift. The uphill battle was done and I reached the pinnacle moment. I could finally enjoy the break from feeling chronically awful. My body began feeling stronger and healthier with each passing day.

Using stress-reducing essential oils, as discussed in the previous chapters, can get you through some aspects of the difficult transition. There are also specific breathing techniques that can assist you through the tough parts. Let's turn our attention now to the topic of meditation and the essential interconnection between the mind and body.

Self-Care S.Y.S.T.E.M.

- The candida-fighting foods mentioned are just the beginning of a cleanse. If you have major overgrowth, consider enrolling in a monitored cleanse program.
- When we eat, we are either fighting candida or feeding it.
- If possible, limit antibiotic use (talk with your doctor) and instead choose natural solutions.
- Be prepared emotionally throughout your candida cleanse.

Share your journey with the #ChooseSelfcare community

Step 4:

Movement

Chapter 7:
More Meditation,
Less Medication

**"If the mind is tranquil and occupied with positive thoughts, the body will not easily fall prey to disease."-
Dalai Lama**

You are probably wondering how meditation is consider movement and why I categorized it in this section. Meditation is the highest form of self-care. It is a means of transforming the mind. When the mind is transformed, amazing changes can be manifested within the body as well. The mind-body connection is a powerful one. Restoring your mind through meditation begins with the breath. Pay attention to how your breath moves throughout your body. You may notice clues about your physical and emotional condition. Several benefits of meditation have been documented:

• Slow breathing and heart rate
• Increased blood flow
• Normalize blood pressure
• Reduced anxiety levels
• Decreased muscle tension
• Increased serotonin production
• Promote healing from chronic illness
• Build self-confidence and self-worth
• Reduce PMS symptoms
• Enhance immune system
• Reduce emotional distress

Breathing is one of our most essential activities, yet most of us forget about it, and until we cannot breathe, we take it for granted. By focusing on our breath, and doing it properly, it can become a powerful tool for us. We are able to slow down our mind and create a relaxed state, which has the byproduct of reducing anxiety or stress levels. Just as important, we can use our breath to increase dopamine levels and provide endorphins to lift our mood.

I would like to share a few examples to get you started. I'll show you how using your breath to invite the mind to relax can bring about lower stress and anxiety levels.

Lion's Breath Technique

This breathing technique was discussed in Chapter 2 with The Burning Bowl Method. I have listed it again here for reference. Lion's Breath relieves tension and stress by stretching your entire face, including the jaw and tongue. Don't worry, I shared my Lion's Breath picture to help you not feel silly or alone. ☺

Instructions:

1) To practice this breath, come to a kneeling position with your butt resting on your feet. Cross your ankles under your seat.

2) Place your hands on your knees. Straighten your arms and extend your fingers.
3) Inhale deeply through your nose.
4) Exhale forcefully through the mouth, making a "ha" sound. As you exhale, open your mouth wide and stick out your tongue as far as possible towards your chin.
5) On the next inhale through the nose, return to neutral face.
6) Repeat 4-6 times. Switch your crossed ankles to the opposite one on top, half way through your repetitions.

Alternate Nostril Breathing (Basic Nadi Shodhana)

Alternate nostril breathing is a great preparation for meditation and can help stop negative self-talk. It is a very calming technique and brings about a reduction in the feelings of stress, tension, and anxiety, while at the same time increasing vitality. The technique balances the left and right brain hemispheres, the nervous system and the hormonal system. It clears the mind and improves concentration and memory.

- Balances the nervous system
- Calms a racing mind

Let's Get Started

For the duration of Alternate Nostril Breathing, you will remain seated in a comfortable position. The best time to practice is on an empty stomach.

- Take your right hand and place the index finger and middle finger down, leaving your thumb, ring finger, and pinky free.
- Inhale deeply through both sides of your nose.
- After a complete exhalation, close the left nostril with your ring finger and slowly inhale through the right.
- At the end of the slow and deep inhalation, close the right nostril with your thumb and slowly exhale through the left. When your lungs are completely empty of breath, fully inhale through the left nostril, close the left, and exhale through the right nostril.
- Continue with this alternating breathing for up to five minutes with a smooth and steady flow of breath as you surrender to the present moment with a relaxed and clear mind.

Heart Balloon Meditation

Another deep breathing technique that gets the helps dissolve anxiety or feelings of panic is the Heart Balloon Meditation. This basic yoga breath leverages the creative power of visualization.

Start by completely relaxing your body. In your mind's eye, visualize a heart-shaped balloon. Give the balloon a color, any color that comes to your mind, and notice that the balloon's string is tied in a knot around a heavy rock.

Take in a very slow, deep breath, and as you do you see that your balloon is filling up. Keep your chest still and allow the incoming air to go right down into your stomach. Feel and watch as your tummy gets bigger. Continue the inhalation until it feels like there is no more space for air anywhere in your body. And now exhale slowly and calmly. Feel your entire body relax as you release that breath.

Gradually increase the length of each inhalation, each one becoming longer and stronger. At the same time, your vision of the heart-shaped balloon is getting so big with each inhalation that it finally lifts that bulky rock and floats effortlessly, high up into the sky.

You should feel lighter and experience a release. This exercise will develop and train your body for correct breathing. The visualization decreases stress in the body and generates a release of endorphins.

Gratitude Pages

If negative self-talk has become a habitual burden, then shifting our mind to focus on gratitude instead will help decrease the intensity of the internal battle. Writing gratitude pages is a simple, meditative technique that can be done practically anywhere.

Start by getting your writing tools ready. Sit in a relaxed position and slowly breathe in deeply through the nose, and exhale out gently and under control. After repeating a few relaxing breaths, bring your focus to the feeling of gratitude. What does gratitude mean to you? It could be gratitude for anything, and nothing is too big or too small. Make a list of everything that flows into your mind that reminds you of thankful blessings. You might be surprised by what you find on the pages when you have finished.

It's a great idea to date these sessions in a private journal so if you feel overcome and overwhelmed on a bad day, you can always look back and receive a little pick-me-up. These mood boosters are like a gentle wave of beautiful blessings that have graced your life. These messages wash our minds in positive energy and instantly neutralize negative thoughts.

Mandala Coloring

In recent years, a meditative technique known as mandala coloring has gained tremendous popularity. A mandala, the Sanskrit word for circle, is a spiritual symbol representing the universe and is used to aid in meditative visualization.

Let's Get Started

You will need to gather crayons, colored pencils, paints, or markers in various colors. There are plenty of adult mandala coloring books for sale and even several free ones online. Make sure to select several different styles of mandalas so that you have several options to choose from when you sit down for this meditation.

Find a nice, quiet and comfortable place where you will not be interrupted. Make sure to turn off your cell phone and minimize any other distractions. You can even choose to play some relaxing music softly in the background. Take a moment to relax your mind and body, and breathe deeply to bring about some stillness. When you feel ready, simply start coloring. Don't focus on perfection—rather just let your mind wander, and follow your intuition as you choose the colors. There is no wrong way to color a mandala.

Once you have finished coloring the mandala, take a moment to appreciate it. Notice how the colors and shapes make you feel. You may even want to record these thoughts in your journal so that you can return to them in other meditations for further reflection.

Self-Care Check-In

What was the most positive and uplifting thought you had about yourself today? Were there any thoughts that were critical of yourself? What tools or visualizations can you use to release those negative thoughts and replace them with positive, gentle, loving statements?

Self-Care S.Y.S.T.E.M.

- Meditation has been proven to provide miraculous healing benefits.
- Developing a focus on the act of breathing overcomes stress and anxiety.
- Use essential oils to help calm the mind.
- Visualizations and gratitude help to defeat negative self-talk and reframe perceptions.
- Even the simple act of coloring can be a powerful form of meditation.
- Keeping a journal to track your thoughts after a meditation will prove beneficial to you.

Got a favorite breathing technique? Share it...
#ChooseSelfcare community

Chapter 8:
The Yoga Effect

"Yoga is a deep well into which we can drench our thirst for balance and wholeness." – *author unknown*

You can certainly find your way out of a depressed lifestyle with exercise. The physiological responses that exercise generates provide a tremendous benefit to overall mood management. It causes the production of endorphins that lift our moods and help stabilize mood swings. The impact that aerobic activity has on mood disorders has been well-documented.[16] As little as thirty minutes of exercise five times a week can greatly affect the health of an individual.

One particular type of exercise that has been proven to deliver the physical benefits of weight reduction and toning the body is yoga. Additionally, yoga brings relief from depression, stress and anxiety symptoms by strengthening the mind along with the body. Always remember to consult your healthcare provider before starting a new exercise program.

A great way to begin yoga is with The Sun Salutations. These are sequences of yoga poses performed in a particular order to build heat in the body. They are often used as warm-up sequences for a yoga practice. Each movement is coordinated with your breath: inhale as you extend, and exhale as you bend.

As a demonstration, I have provided Sun Salutation C below. This sequence will warm up the body and get the endorphins pumping—lifting you out of any mood slump. It is of course always better to attend a live class, taught by a certified instructor, in order to understand the alignment and breathing techniques of each pose. However, I have demonstrated and explained the sequence if you would like to learn how to properly perform it.

On the correct slow, deep breathing cues (explained below), perform this Sun Salutation series two to six times. Make sure to discuss this with your medical provider before beginning any new exercise routines.

Sun Salutation C
1) To begin, come to the front (short end) of your mat.
2) Start in **Mountain Pose** with the hands down by your side and palms facing forward.

Mountain Pose/Tadasana

3) Inhale your arms up to the ceiling, looking up at your thumbs in **Upward Salute Pose.**

Upward Salute Pose/Urdhva Hastasana

4) On the exhale, fold forward at the hips (not the stomach) into **Standing Forward Bend.** Let your descent be an offering of gratitude for this self-care time. Keep the spine straight as long as you

can, then let it softly round into a full forward bend. You can bend your knees to ease the strain on your back. Draw your chin inward and gaze at your legs.

Standing Forward Bend/Uttanasana

5) As you inhale, using a straight spine, lift your chin and chest into **Half Standing Forward Bend**. Place your hands on your knees or on the mat.

Half Standing Forward Bend/Ardha Uttanasana

6) Exhale as you **High Lunge**, stepping your right foot back. Keep your fingertips and left heel on the ground. Reach back through your right heel. Beginners can place the right knee on the ground.

7) Inhale as you step your left foot back, coming into **Plank Pose** (also known as High Push-Up Pose). Stack your shoulders over your wrists with straight arms; your hips in line with your shoulders and feet hip width apart. Spread your fingers and align your wrists directly under your shoulders. Draw back through your heels and lengthen your spine.

Plank Pose

8) Exhale as you lower your **knees** to the floor, keeping your elbows tucked in toward your sides. Keeping your hips lifted off the floor and palms flat, bring your **chest** and **chin** to the floor. Place your chest between your hands.

9) Inhale as you draw your chest forward into **Cobra Pose**, keeping your hands underneath your shoulders. Extend your legs along the floor and un-tuck your toes. Draw your shoulders back and lift your chest slightly. Keep your lower ribs on the floor.

Cobra Pose/Bhujangasana

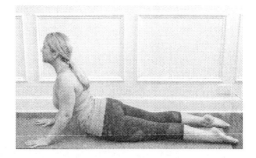

10) While exhaling, tuck your toes under and with a tight core, pull your hips up and back into **Downward-Facing Dog.** Relax your neck. It is okay if you cannot get your feet flat on the mat. If you need to bend your knees, do so. Do what feels good for your body. This is not punishment. Stay here for 5 breaths, focusing on the steady inhalations and exhalations of the breath.

Downward Facing Dog/Adho Mukha Svanasana

11) Inhale as you **High Lunge** stepping your right foot between your hands. Keep your fingertips and right heel on the ground. Reach back through your left heel. Beginners can place the left knee on the ground.

12) Exhale as you step your left foot forward, coming back into the **Standing Forward Fold**. Bend your knees if necessary. Rest your hands beside your feet and bring your nose to your knees.

Standing Forward Fold/Uttanasana

13) With a straight spine, inhale your arms up into **Upward Salute** and look up at your hands.

Upward Salute/Urdhva Hastasana

14) Returning to **Mountain Pose**, exhaling your arms down by your sides.

Mountain Pose/Tadasana

Releasing Strong Emotions

Physically storing emotions for extended periods within our bodies can suffocate our emotional freedom and ability to release. By doing certain poses, we can easily release anger from our hips, sadness from our chest, and stress from our shoulders. Here are a few yoga asanas that can help on an emotional day.

Balasana/Child's Pose

This pose serves as a comforting embrace.

Kneel on the floor with toes together and knees slightly wider than hips. Exhaling, lay your torso down onto your thighs. Reach the arms forward to lengthen them or place the hands back beside the hips to relax shoulders. Soften your heart toward the floor and broaden the shoulder blades as you press them down the back. Let your tailbone lengthen toward the floor.

Benefits:
- Stretches hips, shoulders, and chest

- Relaxes spine and tense back muscles
- Massages the inner organs
- Rejuvenates the body

Modifications:

If your hips do not touch your heels, place a folded blanket under them. A blanket can be placed under the shins to create space for the ankles. Place hands on blocks to deepen the stretch in the chest.

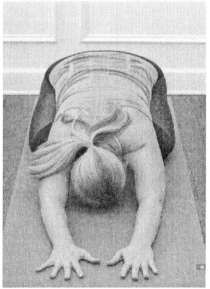

Affirmation: The Universe protects and nurtures me. I am secured and loved.

Viparita Karani/Legs Up The Wall Pose

This pose provides feelings of nourishing, calming, and grounding. It also gives blood circulation a gentle boost toward the upper body, which creates a pleasant rebalancing after you have been standing or sitting for a long period of time. If you are stressed, fatigued, or anxious, this pose is especially refreshing.

Begin by sitting on the floor with a wall next to your side. Your legs should be stretched out straight in front of you. Exhale and gently lie down on your back, then engage your core and hip muscles to bring your legs up into the air with the bottoms of your feet pointing to the ceiling. Pivot your body so the backs of your legs are now touching the wall. Bring your bottom flush to the ground and as close to the wall as possible so your torso and legs create a 90-degree angle.

Relax your neck and focus on your breathing. Stay in this pose for five to 20 minutes. To come out of the pose, gently press the bottoms of your feet into the wall and roll to one side, making sure you support your legs until they reach the ground. Very slowly make the transition to sitting as to avoid lightheadedness.

Setu Bandha Sarvangasana /Bridge Pose

This is a fantastic tension releasing pose. It is one of the best back-bending yoga poses for beginners. It relieves tension in the neck and improves anxiety and stress. Doing bridge pose energizes and rejuvenates while stimulating digestion, thyroid, and lungs.

Lie on your back, knees bent, feet near buttocks and hip-width apart. Slowly lift your lower, middle, and upper back (don't forget to breathe) and raise your hips to the ceiling. Your weight is distributed between your shoulders and feet. Hold the pose. Release by lowering the spine one vertebra at a time. Relax all of your muscles.

Affirmation: I can be vulnerable because I am strong.

Urdhva Dhanurasana/Wheel Pose

This pose is a heart-opener, which helps maintain emotional stability. It is a challenging asana, but stick with it. As you progress in your yoga practice, the wheel pose will become more attainable. Accomplishing the wheel pose will give you a sense of fulfillment and a burst of positivity.

Lie flat on your back. While exhaling, bend the knees and bring the feet as close to the buttocks as possible with the soles of the feet flat on the floor. Bend the arms at the elbows and place the palms of the hands flat on the floor directly under each shoulder with the fingers pointing toward the back. Inhaling slowly, begin to raise the head, back, and buttocks off the floor while arching the spine. Continue to press downward on the hands and feet while raising the hips and stomach as high as possible. Hold the pose for the duration of the held inhaled breath. On the exhale, slowly return the back to the floor, slide the legs straight out and relax.

Kapotasana/Pigeon Pose

Hip openers may be challenging, but they can also be incredibly satisfying, both physically and emotionally. They are great at releasing anger and melting tension.

Begin in Downward-Facing Dog pose. Bring your right knee between your hands, placing your right ankle near your left wrist. Extend your left leg behind you so your kneecap and the top of your foot rest on the floor. Press through your fingertips as you lift your torso away from your thigh. Lengthen the front of your body. Release your tailbone back toward your heels. Work on squaring your hips and the front side of your torso to the front of your mat.

Draw down through your front-leg shin and balance your weight evenly between your right and left hips. Flex your front foot. Press down through the tops of all five toes of the back foot. Gaze downward softly. Hold this position for up to one minute. To release the pose, tuck your back toes, lift your back knee off the mat, and then press yourself back into Downward-Facing Dog. Repeat for the same amount of time on the other side.

The Benefits of Inversions

Yoga uses inversions like Downward Facing Dog and Headstand to reset the parasympathetic nervous system. This helps calm any anxiety and stress that remains physically in our bodies. If this is the beginning of your yoga journey, start with the Downward Facing Dog pose and work your way up to the more difficult ones.

Adho Mukha Svanasana/Downward Facing Dog

Come onto the floor with your hands and knees. With your knees directly below your hips and your hands slightly forward of your shoulders, spread your palms. Exhale as you tuck your toes and lift your knees off the floor. Reach your pelvis up toward the ceiling, then draw your sit bones toward the wall behind you. Gently begin to straighten your legs, but do not lock your knees. Bring your body into the shape of an "A."

Imagine your hips and thighs being pulled backwards from the top of your thighs. Do not walk your feet closer to your hands — keep the extension of your whole body. Relax your neck. It is okay if you can't get your feet flat on the mat. If you need to bend your knees, do so. Do what feels good for your body.

The best way to start with more difficult inversions like the headstand is to use the assistance of a wall until you get the hang of it. Place a foot or tippy-toe against the wall to assist your balance. As you become more confident, you will not need the assistance of the wall as a prop.

Salamba/Supported Headstand

Bring your mat to the nearest wall, placing the shorter edge against it. Standing on your knees (facing the wall), clasp your elbows. Place your forearms to your mat, sliding your palms out to form a triangular shape with your arms. Check to make sure that your palms are about 5-6 inches from the wall (adjusting if necessary). Now interlace your fingers, keeping your palms loose to help ground your wrist and your thumbs pointing toward the ceiling.

Rest the back of your head against the broad base of your thumbs, pressing your crown down into your mat. Now straighten your legs. Keeping your shoulders above your elbows, begin to walk your feet in one at a time until you sense that your hips are directly above your torso. From here, bend both knees, drawing them in to your chest as close as possible and slowly raise them overhead. Use the wall to rest if needed. When ready to come down, slowly bend one knee at a time and bring one leg at a time down to the mat in front of you.

Celebrate the Small Victories

If this all seems too difficult, don't worry! With practice, it will become effortless. I could not even do plank pose for a long time due to a shoulder injury I suffered many years ago. I practiced slowly to get my strength back and within six months, was able to hold a Chaturanga for several minutes hovering an inch above the floor. I celebrated that tiny triumph, and when you have small successes like that, you can celebrate them too!

Self-Care Check-In

Try a pose. How did you feel emotionally and physically afterward? How can you incorporate a daily yoga practice?

Self-Care S.Y.S.T.E.M.

- Don't worry about being a beginner. Start slowly and you will begin to notice the subtle changes.
- There are many different styles of yoga. Try out a few different ones to experience your favorites.
- These are only a few poses to get you started. For a more in-depth practice, attend a local yoga class or visit **www.melissavance.com** for more information.
- Remember to breathe through a difficult pose.
- Celebrate your small yoga victories.

Have a favorite pose? Share your yoga journey with the #ChooseSelfcare community!

Step 5:

Eat Right

Chapter 9:
Craving - Your Body's Way
of Asking for More Self-Care

When I Eat Like Crap, I Feel Like Crap

Food and Its Impact on Mood

Thus far we have addressed how to handle emotional symptoms with essential oils, focused on natural ways to limit our exposure to toxins, and learned how to use moving our minds with meditation and breathing and our bodies with yoga. Adding all of these to our healthier lifestyle will manifest many positive rewards. Let's now take a closer look at the link between our food choices and mood.

Your gut really controls every aspect of your body. You might ask, "How is that possible?" When the balance in your gastrointestinal tract is disrupted, it affects nearly all of the major systems, including those responsible for creating and delivering hormones. Research indicates that up to 95% of the body's serotonin is generated in the intestines. This production is influenced by the bacteria and other microbes residing there.[17]

Serotonin contributes to a feeling of happiness and maintains mood balance. There are indications that a lack of serotonin can lead to symptoms of depression. An imbalance in your gut can be directly responsible for those difficult days. The healthcare of today needs to treat mental health from a root cause perspective, paying special attention to digestion.

95% of our body's serotonin is in our gut.
The gut is the gateway to all disease.

Understanding the importance of our food choices and their direct correlation to our mood is a major milestone, but sometimes it's not that easy. We can have good intentions while planning our healthy meals for the week, but our plan can derailed if an intense craving suddenly overcomes us. In order to be prepared for this, we must understand what cravings are and what they tell us about ourselves.

Cravings Are Signals

Cravings represent a powerful desire for something. Food cravings are the most common type of cravings, yet most of us do not understand what truly makes us crave a type of food.

Self-Care Check In

Do you ever keep eating after you are full? Do you crave salty food? Do you crave sugary food or carb-filled pasta? Do you crave a particular food when you are sad, lonely, or stressed? Why do you think you crave certain foods? The next time you are having a craving, pause and reflect on why this urge is coming up for you. Describe your emotional state and what is going on around you on the following notepad to better understand the catalyst for these cravings.

Before you justify devouring six donuts to satisfy your sweet tooth, we need to discuss what your body is actually asking for. If you crave sugary sweets like candies, cakes, or chocolates, one theory for the reason for your craving is you might be lacking in nutrients such as chromium, phosphorus, sulfur, tryptophan, or magnesium. There are plenty of healthier food options to replenish those missing nutrients to satisfy the cravings. The next time you have a yearning to eat an entire cake, try a few of these nutrient rich foods first:

If you are craving sweets (candies, donuts, cakes, cookies), you might be lacking:
- **Chromium** – sweet potatoes, corn, tomatoes, beets, whole grains, and meat and fish
- **Phosphorus** – whole grains, cottage cheese, peanut butter, chicken, sunflower seeds, and nuts
- **Sulfur** – cruciferous vegetables (broccoli, cauliflower), meat, fish, egg yolks, garlic, and onions
- **Tryptophan** – cheese, yogurt, meat, poultry, legumes, whole grains, nuts, and seeds

- **Magnesium** – raw pumpkin seeds, **dark leafy greens** (spinach, Swiss chard), fish, and beans

If chocolate cravings are your Achilles heel, then take a closer look at your body's magnesium levels. Magnesium is one of the most common nutrients that we are deprived of and could lead to some major health problems. There is a correlation to be found when over 46% of patients diagnosed with cancer are identified to have a magnesium deficiency.[18] Magnesium is found in over 300 different enzymes in the body which are responsible for:

- **Proper bowel function**
- **Heart muscle contractions**
- **Relaxation of blood vessels**
- **Regulation of blood sugar levels**
- **Proper formation of bones and teeth**

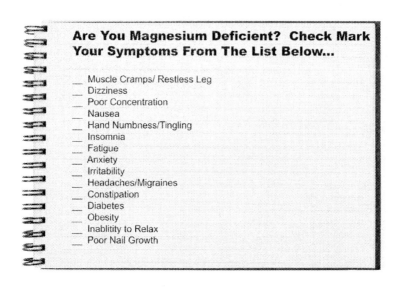

Are You Magnesium Deficient? Check Mark Your Symptoms From The List Below...

___ Muscle Cramps/ Restless Leg
___ Dizziness
___ Poor Concentration
___ Nausea
___ Hand Numbness/Tingling
___ Insomnia
___ Fatigue
___ Anxiety
___ Irritability
___ Headaches/Migraines
___ Constipation
___ Diabetes
___ Obesity
___ Inablitity to Relax
___ Poor Nail Growth

Cravings for Emotional Self-Care

Cravings can hit any person at any time, but the most commonly discussed cravings are the ones that women suffer from specifically. During most women's menstrual cycles, they become overwhelmed with food cravings. When these craving arrive, it is essential to just stop. Take a breath and think. By stopping to consider that it may not be the sweets that your body really wants, you can understand that these cravings may be linked to a B12, vitamin C, or folic acid deficiency.

Lack of the body's nutrients is only one theory for our cravings. We must also consider the emotional cravings that most women's cycles bring forward. A person might, with this knowledge at hand, be able to refrain from making the terrible food choices that never truly satisfy the real reason for the cravings. An intense sugar craving could be signaling the need for emotional self-care.

Emotional eating due to stress, anger, or loneliness is one of the main reasons people want to snack. This coping mechanism becomes destructive when it goes unrecognized. Eating emotionally can quickly spiral out of control, causing many health problems including weight gain and depression. Again, the craving is never truly satisfied and generates a cycle of suffering and poor health.

The next time you have a craving, stop for a minute and scan your emotional health. Are you angry or stressed? Are you sad or lonely or bored? Once you figure out what is wrong emotionally, you can replenish yourself with non-food ways to satisfy the root cause of your cravings.

Diffusing essential oils to calm stressed nerves or uplift a depressed mood could be successful in overcoming an intense sugar craving. Any fulfilling habit could help ease the tension from a craving. Even just taking a brisk walk could help!

Self-Care Check-In

What are some nonfood ways you can satisfy your cravings?

Carb Addiction

Pure sugar is hard to resist. In fact, many people struggle with a long-term sugar addiction that can feed pathogenic candida. The results are digestive disorders, fatigue, mood swings, muscle aches, and much more.

If you are craving sugar—partially due to habitually eating sugar—you should know that this substance is highly addictive. Continuing to reach for sugar to give you the immediate energy boost causes the same physiological response as a cocaine addiction. Eating foods with sugar can cause a massive amount of dopamine to be released creating a surge of activity in the reward centers of the brain. This makes giving up sugar difficult for many. Since sugar is a type of carbohydrate, we should discuss the effect carbs have on our mood.

Observing the euphoric-like state that you may feel when eating simple carbs like pasta and breads can help you detect the link between carbohydrates and mood. When discussing carbs, it is the simple carbohydrates that we need to worry about, like the ones made of white flour and refined sugar. Complex carbohydrates, like whole grains and legumes, take more time for the body to break down and in turn provide more energy – making them the healthier option. If it is pasta you enjoy, there are healthier replacements such as zucchini noodles or quinoa pasta. Recipes for these are in Chapter 10.

A craving for carbs may be a signal of low blood sugar levels. Reaching for more carbs in response will only produce a boost of serotonin. This may temporarily improve your mood, but eventually it will lead to a crash into mood swings and depression. This is the vicious cycle of an addiction to carbs.

Instead of devouring the entire bread basket before your family can get to it (like I used to), focus on eating lean cuts of meat or protein-rich veggies. This will stabilize your blood sugar levels for more extended periods of time. The carb craving is also related to insufficient consumption of good fats, which are crucial for your brain to function properly. One of the best ways that you can introduce some healthy fats into your more nutritious diet would be to incorporate healthy oil-based salad dressings. It is best to make your own when you are putting together your salad, as many of the store-bought ones contain significant amounts of sugar and synthetic junk. For a great example, look to the salad dressing recipe in Chapter 10.

Good Fats:
- Almonds
- Avocado
- Olive Oil

- Coconut Oil
- Salmon

Salty Goodness

An intense craving for salt means that likely essential minerals the body needs to properly function are missing. An effective solution is to choose Himalayan pink salt, which contains the minerals you may be missing. Pink salt is more expensive than regular table salt, but well-worth the investment because it helps to boost your levels of healthy trace minerals while not containing synthetic fillers. It replenishes the minerals you need, thus helping to squelch those pesky cravings you may be feeling for salty snacks. Pink salt won't give you the water retention or health problems to which excessive consumption of regular table salt contributes.

Calcium, magnesium, and zinc deficiencies are all linked to craving salt. Other possibilities could simply be dehydration (check for dark urine as an indicator) or perhaps an indication of underactive adrenal glands. Dark circles under the eyes could illustrate that a person may be consuming too much salt in the diet.

Craving salt is often a learned behavior or habit that you may have developed over years. If you grew up salting your food before tasting it, the food may not taste as good to you when you initially begin consciously cutting back on ingesting salt. However, our taste buds do change and your tastes will soon adjust to the requirement for less salt in your diet.

The wonderful consequence is that you will feel better! We should also be aware that when we regularly eat processed foods, we are already consuming an enormous amount of unhealthy salt. According to Michael Moss, author of SALT SUGAR FAT: How the Food Giants Hooked Us, virtually none of our salt intake comes from the shakers on our table; it comes mostly from ingesting processed food.[19]

Experiencing a sudden lack of sodium may trigger a dopamine reward system in the brain to crave salts. Once we start replenishing the sodium, a biological response occurs, similar to an addiction to crack cocaine. Eating out regularly at restaurants could be unknowingly contributing to your excessive sodium intake. Most restaurants over-salt their dishes with table salt for added flavor, so please be aware when dining out.

Animal Protein Craving

Are you yearning for protein-rich animal foods? It is possible that you might be suffering from a vitamin B, carnitine, magnesium, folate or iron deficiency. Animal-based foods are quite rich in all of these nutrients and minerals. It could also indicate a blood sugar imbalance. Alternatively, it could be a psychological response to instituting too strict of a diet.

At worst, the symptoms could be pointing to anemia, where the blood does not contain enough red blood cells. The most common cause of anemia is a deficiency of iron in the diet. Of course, adding iron-rich foods and supplements to the diet can help to deliver the necessary micronutrients. Using a cast-iron cooking pan can assist, as molecules of iron do process into the food as it is cooked.

Additionally, someone with an iron deficiency should be sure to get plenty of Vitamin C to help the body process the iron. These combined actions can help to overcome the anemia symptoms by addressing the root cause.

Are you concerned about anemia, but still want to eliminate animal proteins from your diet? Try these protein rich vegetables that are high-quality sources for iron:

- Peas
- Asparagus
- Pumpkin Seeds
- Spinach
- Kale
- Nori
- Turnip Greens
- Sea Vegetables
- Tempe
- Kale
- Sesame Seeds

Crave for the Crunch or Tension Eating

Do you find yourself craving crunchy foods like potato chips or pretzels? If so, these could be indicative of inner frustrations. Crunching can give us a minor release of irritation or annoyances. Rather than grabbing the chips, take a moment to focus on your breathing. We have already introduced several breathing techniques that you can call upon. This is a great time to put them to use and release the stress the healthy way.

Here are some healthier options for the "Crunch Effect:"

- Carrot Sticks
- Sliced Peppers
- Baked Kale Chips
- Baby, organic peppers for crunch and snacking

Self-Care S.Y.S.T.E.M.

Tips to Tackle Cravings

- Follow a nutritionally-balanced diet that provides the body a continuous supply of all the essential nutrients.
- Staying hydrated by drinking 8 to 10 glasses of water daily can help keep cravings to a minimum.
- Get plenty of sleep. Sleep deprivation can increase cravings for quick energy foods to keep you awake.
- Engage in activity if you find yourself wanting to eat when not hungry, such as when you are bored or have strong emotional responses.
- If you can't avoid the cravings, limit your portion size to strengthen your self-control muscle, and in time help you avoid over-indulgence.

Chapter 10:
Calm Inflammation

"The Food You Eat Can Be Either The Safest & Most Powerful Form Of Medicine or The Slowest Form Of Poison." - Ann Wigmore

Chronic inflammation stems directly from the choices that we make each day. Poor diet, toxins and stress cause the damaging response within the body. This inflammation is completely reversible when we commit to making better, more informed decisions regarding the foods we eat, the exercise (or lack thereof) that we engage in and the environment in which we surround ourselves. Inflammation is a major factor in virtually all of our health challenges, so we need to hold a specific focus on its reduction as we take action to improve our health.

Common Inflammation Causes:
- Poor dietary choices, such as processed foods, too many animal products, sodas, sugar, excess alcohol
- Food sensitivities
- Lack of movement or exercise
- Gut health issues
- Chronic infections from bacteria, viruses and yeast
- Stress and exhaustion

The body maintains a delicate acid-alkaline balance. When it becomes burdened through poor lifestyle choices, the body has to work even harder to maintain its pH balance. Achieving your desired weight loss goal is so much easier when your body is in a healthy alkaline state.

An acidic body (a body in which organs and systems do not work as efficiently as they should) holds on to excess weight and makes losing that weight difficult. Alkalizing the body with nutrient-rich foods can calm inflammation, which has the byproduct of diminishing pain, increasing energy, and even lifting mood.

Eating an anti-inflammatory diet, and receiving the proper nutrients, such as the omega 3 fatty acids found in fish oil, can radically reduce the symptoms of many illnesses, including depression. Check out the chart below to see if the foods you eat regularly are considered acidic or alkaline.

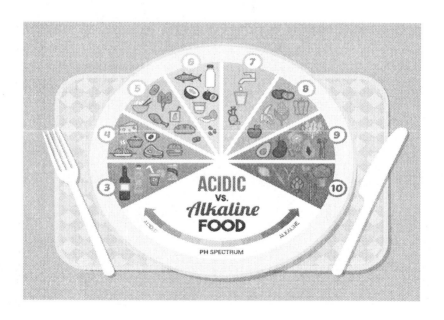

Why such focus on inflammation and an alkaline body? The answer is simple. Disease is triggered by inflammation, which manifests as pain. Inflammation is a vital part of the body's immune response to protect from infection. When the body has too much inflammation, it opens itself up to fall prey to disease. A body can normally fight off a simple cold or allergy, but not when the body is acidic and full of inflammation. This is why it is incredibly important to focus on inflammation and keep the body in an alkaline state when discussing any health concern.

Animal Protein

To decrease inflammation within the body, it is better to limit animal by-products since eating too many of these substances can trigger inflammatory responses in the body. Go veggie heavy. The recipes in this chapter will be plant-based primarily for this reason. You should focus on a mixture of plant-based proteins that together provide all of the essential amino acids, and be assured that you can receive adequate protein intake. Most of us eat far more protein than we actually need.

Daily Protein Requirements Calculation
1) Divide your weight in pounds by 2.2 to get your weight in kilograms.
2) Multiply your weight in kilograms by 0.8 to get the amount in grams of protein you should be eating daily.

The easiest way to get alkaline foods into our diet is through juicing and smoothies. There are many different juice and smoothie combinations you could try that can help your body with pH levels. I have provided a few of my healthy favorites. Try one of these fantastic smoothie and juice recipes or use the notes as inspiration to create your own! Have fun with it!

Let's Get Juicy

Juicing offers many health benefits. It provides a more efficient way to absorb nutrients naturally found in fruits and vegetables. Digestive enzymes are critical components in our digestive process and enable proper absorption of the key nutrients to fight inflammation. As our food becomes more and more processed, its natural supply of enzymes has significantly diminished. As our own natural production of enzyme levels drop significantly with age, supplementing with a good digestive enzyme could be beneficial. With consistent juicing, we can keep those levels near their optimum. Revitalizing our digestive system's ability to take in and utilize nutrients is an important part of our wellness journey.

It is easy to get started with juicing as long as you have a quality juicer. There are two main types of juicers: centrifugal and masticating. It is up to your personal preference which will work best for you. Either type will provide a quality juice to do your body good.

Flu Shot

Juice all ingredients and drink immediately to boost your immune system during flu season.

5 carrots
3 kale leaves
1 celery stalk
1 cup spinach
1 inch of grated ginger
1 inch of turmeric

Wheatgrass Power Shot

This little shot packs a punch. It cleanses the colon and liver, alkalinizes blood, purifies and rebuilds blood cells, neutralizes toxins, and oxygenates cells throughout the body.

Just put the Wheatgrass in your juicer. Pour in a shot glass and drink! If the taste is too much for you (it is for me), chase it with a shot of freshly squeezed apple or orange juice.

Green Juice Shot

For a quick juice shot that packs a nutrient punch!

Ingredients:

6 Kale Leaves
½ Bunch of Parsley
1 Cucumber

4 Celery Ribs
3 small Apples (with skin)
½ Lemon (without skin)

Wash and prepare your fruit and vegetables. Place them in the juicer. Juice all of these items and pour into a glass and drink. Your body will thank you.

Benefits of Blending a Smoothie

If you have access to a blender and good ingredients, making a smoothie is a breeze. The clean-up afterward is much less than what is required with juicing. By blending the fruit and vegetables, you keep all of the fiber content which provides nutrients to keep you feeling full longer than juicing. It is the perfect way to have a meal or snack on-the-go.

Candida-Friendly Smoothie

It is super easy to throw a lot of fruit in a smoothie to make it take extra sweet and yummy, but let's remember to balance out the smoothie with other ingredients so that we don't have a blood sugar spike. It is extra-important to choose low sugar fruits (strawberries, blueberries, peaches, green apples) or no fruit at all if candida is an issue for you.

Popeye's Power

When juiced, leafy greens release high levels of zinc, which are easily absorbed into the bloodstream. Spinach also is high in protein and vitamins A, C, E, K, thiamin, calcium, iron, magnesium, and potassium. You get the idea—spinach packs a nutritious punch.

Instructions:

Blend until smooth...

3 cups organic spinach

1 cup of organic cantaloupe

¼ cup of water or apple juice depending on desired sweetness

Hemp Hemp Hooray Smoothie

The nutrients in bananas increase serotonin levels. The body uses serotonin to regulate mood, appetite, and even sleep. Swiss chard contains vitamin K (used by the body to aid in the absorption of calcium) and magnesium and also serves as an excellent source of calcium. Cherries are a powerful antioxidant and great source of dietary melatonin. Melatonin helps sync the body's natural rhythms, including sleep cycles. Avocado is a healthy fat and will help stabilize blood sugar levels. Lime is high in vitamin C and is extremely beneficial in both cleansing and nourishing the body.

Blend Ingredients:
1 tbsp hemp seeds
1 small frozen banana
1 cup frozen cherries
1 handful of spinach
1 handful of Swiss chard leaves
½ sliced avocado (remove pit)
1 lime, juiced
4-8 oz of water (adjust for desired thickness)

RAW-MOND Milk
Swap the dairy for almond milk since animal protein and products can trigger an inflammatory response within the body.

Ingredients:
2 cups whole raw organic almonds, walnuts, or hazelnuts
Cold water for soaking
Mason jar
Nut-milk bag
Dash of pink Himalayan salt
Date or raw honey for sweetness (optional)
Organic vanilla extract (optional)

Place almonds in a Mason jar and cover with cold water. Refrigerate and soak for 12 hours. Drain the water and place the almonds in a high-speed blender, adding 5 cups of fresh cold water. Blend on a medium speed for about 1 minute. Strain the mixture through a nut-milk bag into a glass container, making sure to squeeze as much liquid from the pulp as possible. Add the salt and sweetener to your liking. Store in the fridge. Be aware since there are no added emulsifiers or preservatives, this milk will only last a few days instead of months.

Purple Power Smoothie
Blend these antioxidant rich ingredients and serve.
1 cup almond milk
¼ cup frozen blueberries
1 banana
¼ cup raspberries

Pineapple Pain Away Smoothie

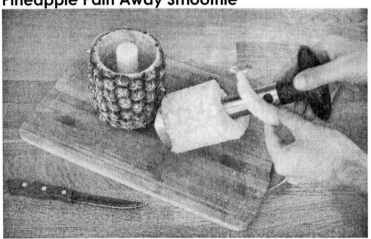

Pineapple contains an enzyme shown to be extremely effective in reducing inflammation in the body. Turmeric and ginger are also two powerful anti-inflammatory roots that have been studied extensively for their pain-relieving properties.

Ingredients:
1 small, ripe pineapple, chopped into cubes
1/2 large cucumber (remove the skin if there is wax on the outside, even if organic)
2 oranges, squeezed for their juice
1 cup coconut water
3 inches turmeric root
2 inches ginger root

Put the above ingredients into a high-speed blender. Blend for 30 seconds and enjoy!

Teas & Tonics

Electrolyte Tonic

This homemade electrolyte tonic replenishes your body from dehydration without harmful artificial colors and synthetic ingredients like most sports drinks on the market.

Ingredients:

½ cup fresh orange juice
¼ cup fresh lemon juice
2 cups of filtered water or raw coconut water
2 tbsp organic raw honey or organic maple syrup
1/8 tsp Himalayan pink salt
Blend all ingredients in a blender and store in glass jar with a lid.

Orange You Glad Tonic
Ingredients:

1 cup coconut water (or filtered water)
1 tbsp grated fresh turmeric (or ½ tsp dried turmeric powder)
1/2 tbsp grated fresh ginger
Juice from 1 orange
1 small carrot
1/2 tbsp raw honey
Pinch of black pepper
Pinch of cayenne

Place all ingredients into high speed blender and blend until smooth. Drink as is or strain before serving.

How to Make Turmeric Tea

Here is a turmeric tea recipe that you might want to try. Feel free to experiment with the ingredients and flavorings until you find a combination that suits your taste.

Turmeric Tea: A Liver Detox
Ingredients:
4 tsp. turmeric
2 tsp. ginger
½ tsp black pepper*
2 tsp cinnamon
1 tsp vanilla extract
2 tsp. raw honey
½ cup of almond or coconut milk
Boiling water

Fill mug halfway with boiling water. Add turmeric, black pepper, and ginger. Cover and let steep for 10-15 minutes. Stir in cinnamon, vanilla, and honey. Fill the rest of the mug with almond or coconut milk and stir. Enjoy!

The benefits of turmeric tea are numerous:
- Detoxes the body
- Boosts immune system
- Protects liver tissue
- Cleanses and purifies the blood
- Eases symptoms of cough and colds
- Improves circulation
- Improves skin
- Reduces inflammation

Nutrient-Packed Recipes

When I introduced the juicer and cutting board into my life, I quickly developed an appreciation for the sound of vegetables being chopped. Soon I began to feel better. I became stronger, less foggy and more alive.

The number one reason most people choose unhealthy fast food is because they feel their busy lifestyle does not allow time for preparation of healthier food. They incorrectly assume that creating nutritious dishes is going to be far more time-consuming. The combination of preparation and time management is key to success in achieving your self-care goals. Preparing food ahead of time, for the week, will not only save you time and money, but also a huge amount of unnecessary calories.

Food Prep Tips:
- Create a weekly menu and have *fun* with this.
- Shop, prep, and cook in the same day (usually a day off from work).
- Use glass containers for grab & go meals.
- Pre-wash and cut veggies and place them in small containers for snacking

Salad In A Jar

There are many different salad in a jar choices that you could make. Pick from several different ingredients: lettuce, spinach, kale, peppers, olives, seeds, nuts, tomatoes, cucumbers, and onions are all fantastic. After washing and chopping your selection of vegetables, place them in a glass jar (Mason jars are my favorite) without the dressing. If you add the dressing to your jar a long time before you are ready to eat, the mixture will become soggy. The idea here is to make several jars and store them in the fridge so they are ready to be grabbed when the time is right.

To mix things up, make one jar a Mexican salad with corn, lettuce, tomatoes, peppers, brown rice, and black beans (you can do a lime and olive oil dressing with sea salt and pepper seasoning of your choice). Or make one jar an Asian-inspired stir-fry with bok choy, carrots, broccoli, edamame, and brown rice (sesame oil dressing works nicely with this).

Preservative Free Salad Dressing

Mix all ingredients and serve over a salad or pour into the bottom of a Mason jar for salad in a jar. Enjoy!

2 Tbsp olive oil
1 juiced lemon
½ tsp pink salt
1 minced garlic clove

A Side of Happiness

My version of Nigella's Happiness Soup.

Ingredients:

3 large yellow squash chopped
Zest and juice of 1 lemon
2 tablespoons olive oil
1 teaspoon turmeric
1 cup vegetable stock (or chicken stock)
½ cup basmati rice
Pink salt and black pepper

Put squash into a pan with lemon zest and olive oil. Stir and cook on gentle heat for about 5 minutes until they are softened. Next, stir in turmeric, broth, and lemon juice. Drop the rice in and cook, uncovered, for about 15 minutes or until the rice is tender. Sprinkle in salt and pepper and serve as a wonderful inflammation-fighting side dish or add more broth to the recipe and serve as a soup. This recipe can be tripled and frozen, to be thawed for later meals when there is no time to cook.

Kale Salad
Ingredients:
3 cups of organic raw kale leaves
1 tsp. of olive oil
1 lemon, juiced
1 tsp. of sea salt

Remove the leaves from the stems of the kale. In a bowl, combine the de-stemmed kale leaves with the remaining ingredients. Using a kneading/massaging action, start to tear the leaves apart and massage. Massage for about 4 minutes or until the leaves are softened. Use this as a salad base or add toppings of your choice.

Guacamole Recipe

Ingredients:
1 ripe Hass avocado
1-2 cloves garlic, chopped
1/2 lemon

1 small handful of cilantro, chopped
Dash sea salt
Dash cayenne pepper

Cut avocado in half lengthwise and remove the seed. Dice avocado flesh. Combine avocado, garlic, cilantro, sea salt and pepper in a bowl and mash together. Squeeze lemon juice into avocado mixture and mix well. Serve with vegetable sticks.

Limit Gluten

Gluten has been known to trigger inflammation within the body, so if the goal is to alkalize the body, it is best to stay away from it. Choosing brown rice and quinoa to replace highly-processed white flour pasta is an excellent way to get whole grains without the toxins. Also, replace that bun with an extra large romaine lettuce or Swiss chard to wrap your sandwiches. It is super-healthy and contains way less calories. Lettuce get started!

Cooking Tip: Brown Rice & Quinoa

Cook extra brown rice and quinoa without added vegetables and store them in the fridge. This way you have them handy to pair with any type of vegetable, which enables you to create an Asian, Mediterranean, or Mexican dish depending on your choice. This saves you time, money, and limits the chance of you choosing junk food if you are starving.

Quinoa Vegetable Melody Recipe
Ingredients:
2 cups cooked quinoa
2 tbsp coconut oil
½ cup thinly sliced scallions
1 tbsp ginger
3 garlic cloves, minced
2 tbsp gluten-free tamari
1 tbsp toasted sesame oil
1 cup finely chopped kale
1 cup diced baby bok choy
1 yellow squash, finely diced
1 cup broccoli florets
1 red bell pepper, finely diced
1 tbsp sesame seeds

Heat a large skillet over medium-high heat. Add 2 tablespoons of coconut oil and garlic, scallions, and ginger, stirring for 1 to 2 minutes. Next add the broccoli, peppers, bok choy and squash. Stir and cook until the vegetables begin to soften. Add the quinoa, tamari, and sesame oil, stirring for about 3 minutes. Stir in the kale a cilantro for a minute, and lastly add the sesame seeds.

Spotlight on Quinoa

Quinoa is a grain, however it contains amino acids and is a great source of complete plant protein. It is high in minerals such as calcium, phosphorus, magnesium, potassium, iron, and zinc. These make it very beneficial in tackling unwanted cravings. Make extra plain quinoa without vegetables or seasoning to store in the fridge for meals throughout the week. When you are ready to warm it up, you can throw in any selection of seasoning or vegetables that match your mood.

*You can make this dish with extra protein by beating an egg and frying it with the Quinoa and vegetables.

Zucchini Noodles

Replacing regular pasta with zucchini noodles is a pretty easy way to sneak more veggies into your meals. All you need is a spiralizer, zucchini, and your favorite pasta sauce or drizzle olive oil on top.

Spice It Up!

Studies have shown saffron spice to be as effective as some anti-depressants.[20] Sprinkle it over your meals for an added mood boost.

Roasted Cauliflower (Pick Your Spice Adventure)
Ingredients (Adventure One):
1 head cauliflower
1 Tbsp. cumin
1 Tbsp. garlic powder
2 tsp. turmeric
2 Tbsp. chili powder
2 tsp. sea salt
1 Tbsp. lime juice
¼ cups coconut milk
½ tsp. black pepper

Ingredients (Adventure Two):
1 head cauliflower
1 Tbsp. cumin
2 Tbsp. chili powder
2 tsp. sea salt

1 Tbsp. lemon juice
¼ cups coconut milk
½ tsp. black pepper

Ingredients (Adventure Three):
1 head cauliflower
1 Tbsp. mustard
1 Tbsp. dill
2 Tbsp. paprika
1 Tbsp. Saffron
2 tsp. sea salt
1 Tbsp. lemon juice
¼ cups coconut milk
½ tsp. black pepper

Preheat the oven to 400 degrees. Grease a baking sheet with coconut oil. Trim the base of the cauliflower, removing the woody stem and green leaves. In a wide medium bowl, combine the coconut milk with the salt, pepper, spices, lime zest and juice. Holding the cauliflower by its base, dunk the cauliflower into the bowl, using your hands to coat the entire head. Place the cauliflower on the prepared baking sheet. Transfer to the oven and roast 40 minutes, or until exterior is dry to the touch. Let the cauliflower cool slightly, then slice into wedges.

Baked Asparagus
Trim ends. Drizzle with olive oil and sprinkle pink salt and pepper. Bake at 425 degrees for 20 minutes. Serve as is (or you can add shaved Gouda cheese as a topping).

Veggie Kabobs with Chimichurri Sauce
Ingredients:
1 Red, 1 Yellow, 1 Green Bell Pepper
1 Yellow Onion
1 Eggplant
1 Yellow Squash
1 Zucchini
2 cups parsley
1 tbsp dried oregano
¼ cup cilantro
5 cloves of garlic
2 tbsp chopped red onion
¾ cup olive oil
2 tbsp red wine vinegar
1 tbsp lime juice
Pink salt & red pepper flakes to taste

Pulse the garlic and red onion in a food processor until finely chopped. Add parsley, oregano, and cilantro and pulse until herbs are finely chopped. Transfer the mixture to a separate bowl and add olive oil, lime juice, vinegar, and stir. Season with pink salt and red pepper flakes. Store in refrigerator until ready to serve over vegetable kabobs.

Sautéed Garlic Kale
Ingredients:
4 cups of kale leaves chopped
2 tablespoons olive oil
1 cloves garlic, finely sliced
1/2 cup vegetable stock or water
Pink salt and black pepper

Heat olive oil in a large saucepan over medium-high heat. Add the garlic and cook until browning occurs. Raise heat to high, add the stock and kale and toss to combine. Cover and cook for 5 minutes. Remove cover and continue to cook, stirring until all the liquid has evaporated. Season with salt and pepper to taste. Makes an excellent side dish.

Self-Care S.Y.S.T.E.M.

- Add more alkaline foods to your daily meals to help fight inflammation.
- Switch out dairy for almond or coconut milk.
- Choose low-sugar juice and smoothies if concerned about candida.
- Food prep for the week.
- Spice up your recipes to keep it unique and fun.
- Go veggie heavy with recipes.

Use #ChooseSelfcare to share pictures of your favorite healthy dishes with our Self-Care Community on Social Media.

Conclusion:
Eat, Live, Connect

Self-Care is How You Take Your Power Back!

This book was meant for you. You are interested in living differently, more naturally, and empowered. You are craving more out of this life. Self-care is a form of compassion towards yourself. It is a type of self-love directed towards your own well-being. If your compassion does not include yourself, it is incomplete. Self-love is making your physical, mental and emotional health a priority. Go back to the end of each chapter and highlight the Self-Care S.Y.S.T.E.M. notes that resonate with you the most. Start a journal and keep track of your daily progress and experiences.

It's Not Just About the Way We Eat, It's Also About the Way We Live.

Honor your pace. If you decide on a cupcake instead of a green smoothie, you still have an opportunity to choose self-care. Choose to not attack yourself for your decision. There is no need for the negative self-talk. Instead enjoy your cupcake guilt-free. Attacking ourselves for not making the best decision in a particular moment will only contribute to our problems and stress. Instead, choose to love yourself, cherish your body and remember...

You Are Allowed To Be Both A Masterpiece and a Work In Progress, Simultaneously

Loneliness can accelerate depression symptoms and other illnesses. Let family and friends know that you are on a self-care journey. Those that want to see you grow will be supportive. Attend a local yoga or meditation class to deepen the skills you were introduced to in Chapter 8 and possibly make new friends.

Use social media to get inspired and connect with others in this self-care journey. Sometimes we need someone to simply be there. Not to fix anything, or to do anything in particular, but just to let us feel that we are cared for and supported. Welcome to your new life in self-care and watch the transformation begin! #chooseselfcare

Become A Priority In Your Life ...

SELF-CARE IS THE NEW HEALTH-CARE®

ChooseSelfcare.com

References

1. Wenjun Zhong, Hilal Maradit-Kremers, Jennifer L. St. Sauver, Barbara P. Yawn, John O. Ebbert, Veronique L. Roger, Debra J. Jacobson, Michaela E. McGree, Scott M. Brue, Walter A. Rocca, "Age and Sex Patterns of Drug Prescribing in a Defined American Population," *Mayo Clinic Proceedings* 88, no. 7 (2013): 697-707, http://www.mayoclinicproceedings.org/article/S0025-6196(13)00357-1/fulltext.
2. The Commonwealth Fund, "U.S. Spends Far More for Health Care Than 12 Industrialized Nations, but Quality Varies," May 3, 2012, http://www.commonwealth fund.org/publications/press-releases/2012/may/us-spends-far-more-for-health-care-than-12-industrialized-nations-but-quality-varies.
3. Larry Trivieri, Jr. and John W. Anderson, eds., *Alternative Medicine: The Definitive Guide* (Berkeley, CA: Celestial Arts, 2002): 81.
4. Tanya Lewis, "Does the Heart Have a Sense of Smell?," *LiveScience*, April 7, 2013, http://www.livescience.com/28498-can-the-heart-smell.html.
5. Rand S. Swenson, *Review of Clinical and Functional Neuroscience*, in: GL Holmes, ed., *Educational Review Manual in Neurology* (New York: Castle Connolly Graduate Medical Publishing, Ltd., 2006).
6. Somrudee Saiyudthong and Charles A. Marsden, "Acute Effects of Bergamot Oil on Anxiety-Related Behaviour and Corticosterone Level in Rats," *Phytotherapy Research* 25, no. 6 (2011): 858-862, http://www.ncbi.nlm.nih.gov/pubmed/21105176.
7. Tapanee Hongratanaworakit and Gerhard Buchbauer, "Relaxing Effect of Ylang Ylang Oil on Humans After Transdermal Absorption," *Phytotherapy Research* 20, no. 9 (2006): 758-763, http://www.ncbi.nlm.nih.gov/pubmed/16807875.

8. Siegfried Kasper, "An Orally Administered Lavandulla Oil Preparation (Silexan) for Anxiety Disorder and Related Conditions: An Evidence Based Review," *International Journal of Psychiatry in Clinical Practice* 17, no. 1 (2013): 15-22, http://www.ncbi.nlm.nih.gov/pubmed/23808618.

9. B Uehleke, S Schaper, A Dienel, S Schlaefke and R Stange, "Phase II Trial on the Effects of Silexan in Patients with Neurasthenia, Post-Traumatic Stress Disorder or Somatization Disorder," *Phytomedicine* 19, nos. 8-9 (2012): 665-671, http://www.unbound medicine.com/medline/citation/22475718/Phase_II_tria l_on_the_effects_of_Silexan_in_patients_with_neurasthe nia_post_traumatic_stress_disorder_or_somatization_dis order_.

10. Jay D. Amsterdam, Justine Shults, Irene Soeller, Jun James Mao, Kenneth Rockwell and Andrew B. Newberg, "Chamomile (*Matricaria recutita*) May Have Antidepressant Activity in Anxious Depressed Humans – An Exploratory Study," *Alternative Therapies in Health and Medicine* 18, no. 5 (2012): 44-49, http://www.ncbi.nlm.nih.gov/pmc/articles/PMC3600408/.

11. Wendell Berry, *Sex, Economy, Freedom & Community: Eight Essays*, (New York: Pantheon, 1993).

12. Dan Shi, Olga Nikodijevic, Kenneth A. Jacobson and John W. Daly, "Chronic Caffeine Alters the Density of Adenosine, Adrenergic, Cholinergic, GABA, and Serotonin Receptors and Calcium Channels in Mouse Brain," *Cellular and Molecular Neurobiology* 13, no. 3 (1993): 247-261, http://www.ncbi.nlm.nih.gov/pubmed/8242688.

13. Tracy L. Parnell and Linda J. Harris, "Reducing *Salmonella* on Apples with Wash Practices Commonly Used by Consumers," *Journal of Food Protection* 5, (2003): 741-747, http://www.ncbi.nlm.nih.gov/pubmed/12747679

14. Charles Partito, "Candida Albicans," *Ejuva*, April 7, 2011, http://www.ejuva.com/blog/candida.html.

15. Amy Myers, "Anxious? Moody? Depressed? Why You Might Have Candida," *MindBodyGreen*, June 18, 2014, http://www.mindbodygreen.com/0-14177/anxious-moody-depressed-why-you-might-have-candida.html.
16. James A. Blumenthal, Patrick J. Smith and Benson M. Hoffman, "Is Exercise a Viable Treatment for Depression?," *ACSM's Health & Fitness Journal* 16, no.4 (2012): 14-21, http://www.ncbi.nlm.nih.gov/pmc/articles/PMC3674785/
17. Jessica M. Yano, Kristie Yu, Gregory P. Donaldson, Gauri G. Shastri, Phoebe Ann, Liang Ma, Cathryn R. Nagler, Rustem F. Ismagilov, Sarkis K. Mazmanian and Elaine Y. Hsiao, "Indigenous Bacteria from the Gut Microbiota Regulate Host Serotonin Biosynthesis," *Cell* 161, no. 2 (2015): 264-276, http://www.caltech.edu/news/microbes-help-produce-serotonin-gut-46495.
18. Mark Sircus, "A Magnesium Deficiency Increases Cancer Risk Significantly," *Natural News*, May 21, 2008, http://www.naturalnews.com/023279_magnesium_cancer_calcium.html
19. Michael Moss, *Salt Sugar Fat: How the Food Giants Hooked Us*, (New York: Random House Trade Paperbacks, 2014).
20. AL Lopresti and PD Drummond, "Saffron (*Crocus sativus*) for Depression: A Systematic Review of Clinical Studies and Examination of Underlying Antidepressant Mechanisms of Action," *Human Psychopharmacology* 29, no. 6 (2014): 517-527, http://www.psychcongress.com/article/saffron-effective-some-antidepressants-19359.

Photo Credits

Front Cover Photo taken by Lisa Sanders,
Photos inside the chapters courtesy of Dollar Photo Club and Shutterstock,
Yoga poses from Chapter 8 and back cover courtesy of Jennifer Bonti with Jenny Bee Photography,
About the Author photo taken by Priscila Camara

Notes

Acknowledgements

This book would have never happened if not for the unwavering support of my family, friends, and yoga tribe, who cheered me on when I had played with self-doubt. I must give special thanks to Karen Thomas and Tanya Hanna for the gentle reminders of how much the world needs this book. I am also thankful for my mentors from The Institute for Integrative Nutrition®, who have opened so many doors for me. I am truly blessed to have the encouragement of my Taekwondo Master Dongmin Choi, who taught me to always "finish what you start."
I am eternally grateful for my husband, David Vance, who loved me when I was at my most unlovable. When I was so chronically ill all those years ago, he picked up the slack without complaint.

"Only In The Darkness Can You See The Stars."
   – Martin Luther King Jr.

I feel immense gratitude to the team of individuals who encouraged and uplifted me through this liberating yet disturbing process of writing and publishing a book. Thank you to Gina Fontana for the cover illustration; Jennifer Bonti with Jenny Bee Photography for capturing wonderful yoga photos; Lisa Sanders with Lisa Sanders Photography for the cover shot; Priscila Camara Photography for the family photo on the inside back cover; Rupa Limbu for cover design; Paula High for her valuable suggestions; and Greg Adkins with New Frame Creative for web development and creating a beautiful logo for my business. I'm so grateful for all of the time and hard work you all contributed to the success of this book.

Share the Love

Thank you so much for reading this book and allowing me to share in your journey. When I set out to make a career in wellness, I always hoped to have a positive impact on people's lives, but I never imagined having the wide reach that writing a book would give me. The truth is, there are still so many people out there that are struggling. It doesn't take much looking to see a world that is in pain. If you enjoyed this book and felt that its message helped you heal in some way, please consider leaving a review on Amazon. The more reviews, the bigger the reach, and the more people that, like you, can have their lives changed by what they read. Again, thank you, from the very bottom of my heart.

Sincerely,
Melissa

Work with Melissa

Speaking Engagements & Workshops
Interested in having Melissa speak at your next event? Sample topics include:
- Mindfulness Meditation For Beginners
- Self-Care's Effect on Productivity
- The Bitter Side of Sugar
- Self-Care S.Y.S.T.E.M Goal Setting
- Wellness at Work (Stress Reduction & Office Yoga)
- Goal-Setting and Intentions

Melissa is also able to develop custom workshops according to the needs and interests of your organization.

Corporate Wellness
Be an employer who cares...empower your team to live healthier, happier, and more productive lives by equipping them with powerful self-care information.

Having once juggled a very demanding schedule in the corporate world for many years, she understands the benefits to an organization when its employees are happy and healthy. Today's professionals are in need of health and wellness more than ever before. Employees who are happier and healthier will yield higher productivity, focus, lower health care costs and reduce employee absenteeism.

As your Corporate Wellness Coach, she can work with your HR team to devise a program that fits your corporate culture. Melissa offers speaking, educational workshops, and group coaching as your organization requires. Visit **MelissaVance.com** for more info.

Choose Selfcare

Stay Tuned...

Become a priority in your life.

Blog
Podcast
Journal
Gifts

podcast

Join the mailing list
ChooseSelfcare.com/newsletter

"My passion in life is to not only inspire people to live happier, healthier, and more satisfying lives but more importantly, to teach them how to do it! This passion of mine was ignited after experiencing my own health crisis many years ago. The suffering my family and I experienced was something that was easily corrected by subtle changes, but I needed the knowledge and support in order to break through. After regaining my health and energy through this devastating experience, I added more credentials to my education. This equipped me with extensive knowledge in holistic nutrition, meditation, yoga, and preventative health. My goal is to help clients blast through barriers, stop unnecessary suffering, and ignite positive lifestyle breakthroughs. I do this by creating engaging programs and actionable digital content while providing practical advice and achievable strategies through personal coaching." – Melissa

CONNECT WITH ME

@CHOOSESELFCARE

Melissa resides in Alpharetta, Ga with her husband and two children